THOREAU ABROAD

Twelve Bibliographical Essays

THOREAU ABROAD

Twelve Bibliographical Essays

Edited by

EUGENE F. TIMPE

With a Foreword by WALTER HARDING
Secretary and Past President, The Thoreau Society

ARCHON BOOKS
1971

©1971 THE SHOE STRING PRESS, INC.
Hamden, Connecticut 06514
Library of Congress Catalog Card Number: 71-146512
International Standard Book Number: 0-208-00401-7

PS
3054
.T5
1971

Printed in the United States of America
All rights reserved

Contents

FOREWORD, Walter Harding, 1

INTRODUCTION, Eugene F. Timpe, 11

A HUNDRED YEARS OF *Walden*, William Condry, 23

THOREAU IN FRANCE, Maurice Gonnaud and Micheline Flak, 31

THOREAU AND VAN EEDEN, Seymour L. Flaxman, 55

THOREAU'S CRITICAL RECEPTION IN GERMANY,
Eugene F. Timpe, 73

HENRY D. THOREAU IN SWITZERLAND, Dominik Jost, 83

THOREAU IN ITALY, Agostino Lombardo, 93

THOREAU'S INFLUENCE IN BOHEMIA, Otakar Vočadlo, 117

THOREAU IN RUSSIA, Jerzy R. Krzyzrnowski, 131

THOREAU AND ISRAEL, Sholom J. Kahn, 141

THOREAU IN INDIA, Sujit Mukherjee, 153

THOREAU IN JAPAN, Katsuhiko Takeda, 165

THOREAU IN AUSTRALIA, Joseph Jones, 183

Acknowledgments

Financial support at various times during the long gestation period of this work from the Research Office of the College of Liberal Arts of The Pennsylvania State University is gratefully acknowledged.

The editor is grateful to those who have given permission to print the following essays:

Mouton & Co. for portions from E. F. Timpe's "The Macrocosm of *Walden*," from *Actes du IVe Congrès de l'Association Internationale de Littérature Comparée*, I, pp. 73–79, used in the Introduction.

Dublin Magazine, for "A Hundred Years of *Walden*" (reprinted without alteration from the original in Volume XXXI [1955], pp. 42–46).

Der Friede, for Thoreau and van Eeden," (a revision of "Thoreau and van Eeden," [1961], pp. 341–352)

The Thoreau Society Bulletin, for "Thoreau's Critical Reception in Germany," (a revision of "Thoreau in Germany," XCIII [1965], pp. 1–3)

Neue Zürcher Zeitung, for "Henry D. Thoreau in Switzerland," (a translation and revision of the article originally written for *Thoreau Abroad* but published earlier as "Henry D. Thoreau und die Schweiz," [9 July 1967]).

Foreword

Walter Harding

WALTER HARDING is University Professor of English at The State University of New York campus in Geneseo throughout the academic year and teacher of the Thoreau Seminars in Concord during the summers. He is the Secretary and past President of the Thoreau Society. Included among his many books on Thoreau are *A Thoreau Handbook* (1959), *Thoreau: Man of Concord* (1960), *The Days of Henry Thoreau* (1965), and *Thoreau's Turtle Nest* (1967). In addition, he is the Editor-in-Chief for the Modern Language Association edition of *The Works of Henry David Thoreau*. As United States State Department Lecturer he has spoken on Thoreau in Japan, Iceland, Norway, Spain, France, and Germany.

FOREWORD

I

The growth of Henry David Thoreau's reputation in the century since his death is one of the most startling phenomena in American literature. In his own lifetime and, indeed, for a quarter of a century afterwards, he was almost universally dismissed as a second-rate imitator of Ralph Waldo Emerson. Neither of the two books he succeeded in getting published during his lifetime—*A Week on the Concord and Merrimack Rivers* (1849) and *Walden* (1854) was a success. Indeed, the former sold fewer than two hundred copies in its first four years and the unsold stock was returned to the author as unsaleable, while the latter took five years to sell out the small edition of two thousand copies. Both books were out of print at the time of the author's death in 1862—though, ironically, both were brought back into print within a few months of that event. Despite the fact that five more volumes of his works were published in the four years after his death, the sales of his works then can hardly be described as phenomenal. It was sufficient to keep all seven volumes in print over the years, but that was about all.

The first serious widespread interest in his works came in the last decade of the nineteenth century and was sparked chiefly by a general rise in interest in natural history and, concomitantly, in writings about nature. By a fortunate coincidence, Thoreau's friend and literary heir, Harrison Gray Otis Blake, had in the 1880's and early 1890's edited a series of excerpts from Thoreau's then unpublished journals in four volumes—*Early Spring in Massachusetts* (1881), *Summer* (1884), *Winter* (1888), and *Autumn* (1892)—which were devoted almost entirely to his comments, arranged in calendar form, on the natural history of Concord. These volumes served to call attention to Thoreau as a nature writer and thus helped to popularize his other books.

With the exception of a minute trickle of interest in England, there had been, up to this time, not the slightest indication of any enthusiasm for Thoreau outside his native country. Then suddenly in the 1890's, editions, translations, critical articles, and even biographies began to appear in various European countries such as England, Ireland, Holland and Germany. Some of this new interest was due to that pioneer critic Henry Stephens Salt of England who also, incidentally, was responsible for arousing a similar interest in Thoreau's then equally forgotten contemporary, Herman Melville. Salt was years ahead of his time in many fields and the interest he stirred up I think we can consider to be somewhat atypical. But outside the Salt-stimulated excitement, if I may call it that, the interest was primarily in Thoreau as a nature writer and I think it significant that it was most prominent in Germany where an interest in the out-of-doors is traditional.

But this interest in Thoreau at the turn of the century was a transitory one and for almost half a century afterwards he was, practically speaking, a forgotten man once more outside his own country. (To be perfectly truthful, he was also pretty much a forgotten man there, too.)

The real surge of interest in Thoreau both at home and particularly abroad came after World War II. Translations began to appear seemingly everywhere, in such places as Denmark, Sweden, Norway, Finland, Switzerland, Germany, Russia, France, Spain, Italy, Greece, Israel, Argentina, Brazil, Taiwan, Japan, and India. He who a century ago had been dismissed as a failure became, hardly an international household name, but unquestionably a name to be reckoned with in intellectual circles around the world. The late Henry S. Canby used to tell the story of hearing a little Australian girl, daughter of a Thoreau enthusiast, cite the major bodies of water in the United States as "the Great Lakes, the Mississippi River,—and Walden Pond" and while her geography might be a little off, there was something to be said for her case.

I have had the good fortune of serving as secretary of the Thoreau Society since its establishment in 1941. Originated as a clearing house for American Thoreau scholars, it very rapidly became a center for Thoreau enthusiasts in all walks of life. But what is more interesting is that with no attempts at proselytizing on the part of the society, it has gradually developed into an international society with active subsidiary societies in Japan, England, and France and with members in Norway, Denmark, Belgium, Spain, Italy, West Germany, Yugoslavia, Israel, Lebanon, India, Australia, Argentina, and Uruguay. News of the society has spread simply by word of mouth from state to state and from country to country. And I regularly receive unsolicited letters from the proverbial four corners of the earth expressing enthusiasm for Thoreau and inquiring how one may become a member of the society. Excerpts from three such letters will show the width of their range:

From England:

> I have no education save what I have garnered since leaving school. . . . In 1954 I met [Thoreau] and have read him constantly since. . . . Each year I get more from him, yet find it difficult clearly to express why he is so exciting and stimulating to me. . . . I came upon *Walden* to find my wildest beliefs confirmed. Surely he is one of the greatest men who ever lived.

From Cameroon:

> I found Thoreau in the USIS Library in Lomé-Togo. There is much philosophical wisdom in Thoreau's literature that must be seriously emulated, if a happier world is envisaged. In these hard times, the ideals and voices of this lonely evangel should be better known.

And from behind the Iron Curtain, in Yugoslavia:

> I am interested in all details regarding Thoreau's work, life, philosophical position, etc. Among his works I am mainly interested in *Walden* and "Life without Principle." I have read both books but unfortunately the complete library of work of Thoreau is neither known nor accessible in our country.

It has also been my good fortune to travel in recent years through Japan, Iceland, Norway, Spain, West Germany, and France, lecturing on Thoreau in various colleges and universities under the auspices of the United States Department of State. All told, I have spoken at nearly seventy such institutions and it has been an enlightening experience to see the seemingly almost universal interest in the life and writings of Thoreau.

One incident in particular stands out in my mind. As I have said elsewhere:

> One of the high points of my visit [to Japan] was reached in Sendai. I arrived in the city in mid-afternoon after an 8-hour train journey completely across Honshu from Akita. I had been up late the night before attending a formal dinner and had been traveling at a steady pace for 6 weeks, rarely staying more than 2 days in any one city and sometimes giving two or more lectures in a day. I got off the train to discover I had been scheduled almost immediately to lead a discussion on transcendentalism at the cultural center. I was tired and worn out. My brain refused to function, and for once I seemed unable to get the discussion off the ground. Fortunately I had some colored slides of scenes of the Thoreau country around Concord, Mass., and in desperation I dragged them out and had them flashed on the screen. The audience seemed to enjoy them, and thus I was able to feel that the afternoon had not been completely unrewarding for them, but I was for once depressed and discouraged.
>
> Just before I went up on the platform someone had told me that Professor N——— wanted to see me afterwards. I had no idea who he was, but I agreed to meet him. As soon as the discussion was over, he came up and introduced himself as a member of the faculty of one of the local universities. He went on to explain that during the war he had lost all his possessions in the bombing raids, including a large library that had been the joy of his life. Just one book survived—a copy of Thoreau's *Walden*. He had never read it before, but now when he started on it, he found a whole new world opening before him. In *Walden* Thoreau had said, "How many a man has dated a new era in his life from the reading of a book," and it had proved to be just such a book for Professor N———.
>
> In the years since the war, he had purchased and read every

other book he could find by or about Thoreau. He had with him that afternoon one of those cavernous Japanese briefcases filled with twelve of his most precious volumes, and under his other arm, wrapped in the inevitable Japanese furoshiki (scarf), were another twelve. Note slips bristled out of each volume like quills on a porcupine's back. For years he had been waiting hopefully to find an American who could answer his questions about Thoreau. As he phrased it so expressively, "I have reached the door of the shrine, but the language barrier has kept me from entering it." As a matter of fact, it had not. It was obvious to me in a few minutes that he had absorbed and assimilated Thoreau's philosophy completely. He flipped through the pages of his books from note slip to note slip, asking question after question. Occasionally a colloquialism had tripped him up or puzzled him, but in far more cases his notes showed a profound insight into even the subtleties of Thoreau's philosophy.

We talked for two hours steadily, and, in the face of his contagious enthusiasm, I rapidly forgot all my discouragement and depression. We met again the next morning at my hotel and talked for another two equally exciting hours.

If my lecture later that day at Tohoku Gakuin College in Sendai was one of my most successful, it should be credited to Professor N———'s ebullient revitalization of spirits. Through my work as secretary of the Thoreau Society and through my lectures on Thoreau I have met hundreds of Thoreau enthusiasts. Professor N———'s radiated joy and excitement over the Sage of Walden led them all. It was worth the journey halfway around the world to meet him.

I have already spoken of the widely varied interest in Thoreau. He appeals to many different people for many different reasons. This fact was brought home to me very strikingly when I compared the interests of the Thoreauvians I had met in Japan with those I met in the various European countries. The Japanese look upon Thoreau primarily as a nature writer and an exponent of quiet contemplation in the Zen tradition. The Europeans, on the other hand, think of him as a political activist who fought against slavery in America and who offers a highly workable methodology for today's battle against the forces of tyranny and dictatorship. *Walden* was the Japanese Thoreauvians' bible; "Civil Disobedience," the Europeans'. (Interestingly, many Europeans were astonished that the American State Department would sponsor a lecture tour devoted to such an outspoken rebel against all authority and the fact that it was done, I believe, gave them a new insight into the democratic ideology.)

Those represent only two of the many approaches to Thoreau. It hardly needs saying that he is looked upon as one of the great prose masters of the world. But he is also admired as one of our earliest conservationists, a pioneer ecologist, an authority of the flora and fauna of New England, a mountaineer, a student of the American Indian and his artifacts, an advocate of universal religion, a scholar of the Greek and Roman classics, and a proponent of many other wide and varied causes.

II

Oddly enough, despite the mass of evidence of Thoreau's widespread influence abroad, there has hitherto been little attempt to survey or evaluate that influence. I became very much aware of this hiatus in Thoreau scholarship when I wrote my *Thoreau Handbook* ten years ago, and as a result, devoted about eight pages of that book to a rather hasty survey of the field. The only articles I could find at that time on that subject were Randall Stewart's "The Growth of Thoreau's Reputation," in *College English* in 1946; Gilbert P. Coleman's "Thoreau and His Critics," in *The Dial* of 1906; and one devoted solely to *Walden* entitled "100 Years of Walden," by Francis B. Dedmond in the *Concord Journal* in 1954. There were few articles devoted to his influence in specific countries. Since then some other such specialized articles have appeared, but this book is the first attempt to make a fairly comprehensive study of Thoreau's influence in several foreign countries.

A study of the influence of Thoreau abroad is important for a number of reasons. In the first place, we must recognize, although rather shame-facedly, that for many years Thoreau was a prophet without honor in his own country and that his first general recognition was obtained not here but in England in the latter years of the nineteenth century. More specifically, the significance of his essay on civil disobedience was recognized almost everywhere else before it was here. While we here were still speaking of *Walden* as Thoreau's only masterpiece, he was much more widely known abroad as the author of "Civil Disobedience." Such a survey as this volume is, then, will give us some clues as to why we were so slow to recognize Thoreau's genius—or why others recognized him before we did.

Second, as I have already commented, the diversity of approaches to Thoreau's works is amazingly wide. No two people seem to be attracted to him for exactly the same reasons. His admirers think of him as a litterateur, a naturalist, a political scientist, an economist, an advocate of the simple life, an excursionist, and so on. Foreign admirers of Thoreau have turned up facets of his appeal that Americans have never discovered.

Third, foreign criticism of Thoreau is of value because it helps us to understand attitudes of other peoples toward America, despite the fact that Thoreau is not necessarily considered to be a typical American—though perhaps it might be better for us if he were, because in some respects no other American better represents the tenets of American idealism as expressed in the Declaration of Independence. Foreign critics in many cases have been more aware of that kinship between Thoreau and his political forefathers than have Americans. What Gay Wilson Allen has said of a similar study of the foreign influence of Walt Whitman could just as appropriately be applied to Thoreau; that is, "In view of the increasing importance—and responsibilities—of the United States in world affairs, these foreign critics . . . may help Americans to understand themselves, to understand the misconceptions about themselves that they must overcome, and perhaps ultimately to have a better appreciation of the role their culture can play in the survival of their civilization." Thus Mr. Timpe's volume, I feel, is fulfilling a real need.

Introduction

Eugene F. Timpe

EUGENE F. TIMPE is Associate Professor of German and Comparative Literature at The Pennsylvania State University. His interests have been principally in American-German literary relationships, certain German, English, and American authors, and criticism in regard to style and structure. An early interest in Thoreau was renewed while he was doing research for his dissertation in Vienna in 1959. Comments by early German critics sent him back to the writings of Thoreau himself. The apparent and immediate result was several short studies on Thoreau; then at the International Comparative Literature Association Meeting in Fribourg in 1964 he met Claudio Gorlier (mentioned in Lombardo's essay), Dominik Jost, and Katsuhiko Takeda. He found that they shared his enthusiasm for Thoreau, and at this point it seemed evident to him that their mutual interest should result in a volume such as *Thoreau Abroad*.

INTRODUCTION

In an age of constant reassessment, it is inevitable that one who long ago foresaw our modern dilemma and raised so many of the questions which now preoccupy us should come to be regarded as a sage. If, in addition to dealing with such subjects, in the largest sense, as ecology, the preservation of individuality in an increasingly complex and technical society, the means of dissidence, and the urgency of personal reform, he produced in the process what must be universally regarded as masterpieces of literature, then his legacy is doubly sanctified. That Thoreau has attained of late such a state of prophetic and literary beatification seems hardly open to question. Although scarcely known for many years after his death he has, in the past several decades, come into his own both as a popular idol and as an author whose worth is acknowledged by students and specialists alike. Dissertations are written on him, a Thoreau society was formed by his admirers in 1941, he finds his way into cartoons, he is quoted in motion pictures, his words have become a part of the American idiom, his major writings have been regularly issued and then reissued, and since 1906 even his *Journal* has been in print.

It has been his fate, however, to be taken piecemeal. First he was read as a nature writer and his social philosophy, not to mention his personal beliefs, was ignored. After the great depression this was no longer the case, but still, those who read him often sought verification for their own ideas rather than understanding of his. As a result, he has been cited, at one time and another, in support of an ungodly variety of eccentricities, all of which may be adduced in narrow context from his works but none of which fails to do violence to his total thought. Now at last there is reason to hope that the mass of scholarship, the public interest, the perspective of time, and the multitude of counterbalancing and sometimes conflicting ideas which his work in extraction has been used to support will result in a balance and breadth that will restore his image to a shape not too unlike that which he himself would have approved.

In this process of rectification, students of him have pieced together knowledge on fronts which have gradually become both deeper and broader. From the crude beginning in 1848 by James Russell Lowell when Thoreau was deprecated for his alleged indebtedness to Emerson, criticism has gradually moved into studies of texts, biography, society, sources, themes, symbols, and influences, as well as into every other avenue through which scholars seek to come to terms with a writer and his ideas.

One of these avenues leads to knowledge of the reputation, fame, or reception of an author. A few studies of this sort have previously been published, and in them his acceptance in his own country and, in one or two instances, elsewhere, has been traced. The fact that more work of this kind seemed to be needed engendered the idea of producing this collection. Knowing how a writer is seen outside the context of his own milieu, scholars can sometimes find approaches to him which result in new interpretations. Such information can also provide a basis for assessments of influence. Of course, for a variety of reasons, influence is a vexed question. Thoreau's case illustrates one of these: can an author be said to influence others when it is not merely possible but likely that he simply evokes responses of kindred feelings by striking pre-existing, sympathetic cords? Even in the well-known case of Gandhi and the Indian revolt, Thoreau seems merely to have expressed ideas which already existed in latent form and then to have provided guides to their implementation. Perhaps, then, the question may be restated, not as How much did Thoreau influence others? but as Which of their own dormant dispositions did others discover in him? Yet even such a limited question, if its answer is to be sought in an international frame of reference, depends for a valid answer on knowledge of a number of tangible matters: Which works were translated from the author's canon? How well did the translations represent him? When and to what extent were they made available? How well were they known, both by critics and the general public? and so on. Knowledge of these and many other facets of the case is essential before conclusions can be drawn. Hence this book takes an initial step, especially through the bibliographical material in which it is so rich, in the process of evaluating the effect our author has had in cultures foreign to his own.

There remains, of course, after the skeletal facts have been exposed, the abiding question of "why?" Various answers are suggested or implied by the contents of the essays in this book. One more, however, is worth adding. It is based on the concept that the coin of influence has a reverse side, that the action had an equal and opposite reaction; in a word, Thoreau's acceptance abroad may very well be based on both his provinciality and his cosmopolitanism. The former was attractive to foreign readers because it was fresh from the New World and unfamiliar. The latter, a quality not so apparent in him, was a reflection of the culture of the world at large and as such a subliminally familiar matter to his audience abroad. The combination of the foreign and the vaguely recognizable, as seen from afar, has very likely been an important factor in the fortunes of Thoreau's ideas outside his own land.

That which was foreign in him to others, his provinciality, has long been recognized; his cosmopolitanism has not. Insofar as it is possible to divorce the apparent life of the man from the content of his ideas, it is possible to distinguish a wide gap between the provinciality of his outer life and the cosmopolitanism of part of the inner. Certainly the soil which was not for "the citron and the rose, but for the whortleberry, the pine, or the heather" (as Margaret Fuller said in a letter of rejection for one of Thoreau's poems which he had submitted to the *Dial*, as cited by Walter Harding and Carl Bode in *The Correspondence of Henry David Thoreau*, New York, 1958, p. 56) offered nutrients for some other growths, even if they were exotic for Concord. To find Thoreau cultivating the bloom of cosmopolitanism in his New England garden, although surprising, would not be inconsistent with his character, the essence of which was contradiction. As Ethel Seybold said in her *Thoreau: The Quest and the Classics* (New Haven, 1951), he was

> a partial, intermittent, temporary hermit, who spent a good part of two years in semiseclusion, who rather liked to eat out, who said of himself even, "I am naturally no hermit" (*Writings*, II, 155); a naturalist whose ornithology was never quite trustworthy and who contributed no new fact of importance to natural history; a scholar who believed that men had a respect for scholarship much greater than its use and spoke of the great reproach of idle learning; a classicist who preferred the agricultural writers to the literary authors; a reader of oriental philosophy who genuinely disapproved of any system of philosophy; a student of New England history who found genealogy ridiculous and the facts of history unimportant; an expert on the North American Indian whose experience came largely from books, from Joe Polis, and from gathering arrowheads while the red man still roamed the West; a primitivist who might talk of devouring a raw woodchuck but who also talked of abstaining from animal food; a man of letters who published little and was relieved when it did not sell; a writer who believed that a man's life was the perfect communication; a walker of whom Emerson said that if he did not walk he could not write but who spent his last months in composition and never even referred to his former outdoor life (pp. 1–2).

For such a man the striking of a balance between personal provincialism and intellectual cosmopolitanism was more than merely possible.

If cosmopolitanism meant nothing more than traveling to foreign lands, there would be little hope of finding any of it in Thoreau. Its definition, however, contains the concept of an allegiance to mankind as a whole. This part of the definition parallels one of Thoreau's central aims so closely that it seems almost to be a restatement of it. This aim was to present a universal code or standard of living against which men could hold their lives to measure. And along with this broad allegiance comes as its corollary the rejection of provincial prejudices and narrow loyalties such as those integral to nineteenth-century New England Yankeeism. Thoreau's disavowal of a mean life, in New England or anywhere else, is part of the central theme of his *Walden*, and of super-patriots he wrote "They love the soil which makes their graves, but have no sympathy with the spirit which may still animate their clay. Patriotism is a maggot in their heads" (*Walden* [New York, 1962], pp. 341–342). Finally, in a more concrete sense of the term, cosmopolitanism encompasses the use of materials from other times and places. Strangely enough, Thoreau was largely dependent upon outside materials. Henry Seidel Canby, in his *Thoreau* (Boston, 1939), observed that "His ideas are all borrowed; the originality is in the blending" (p. 151) and Thoreau himself noted in his *Journal* "I do not the least care where I get my ideas, or what suggests them" (*Writings*, Boston, 1906, VIII, 135). Even in comparison with the other transcendentalists Thoreau was eclectic; his writings contain more than occasional references to the literatures, religions, and philosophies of both eastern and western civilizations.

Lest it seem that Thoreau's cosmopolitanism was entirely divorced from an interest in travel itself, it should be noted that evidence of such an interest is spread throughout his works. "I am," he said, "refreshed and expanded when the freight train rattles past me, and I smell the stores which go dispensing their odors all the way from Long Wharf to Lake Champlain, reminding me of foreign parts, of coral reefs, and Indian oceans, and tropical climes, and the extent of the globe. I feel more like a citizen of the world at the sight of the palm-leaf which will cover so many flaxen New England heads the next summer, the Manilla hemp and cocoa-nut husks, the old junk, gunny bags, scrap iron, and rusty nails" (*Walden*, pp. 193–194). As shown in a tally made by John Christie and presented in his "Thoreau, Traveler" (Duke University, Ph. D., 1955), Thoreau mentioned more than 443 foreign locales in his writings (pp. 18–19n). One of the many paradoxes about Thoreau, according to Christie, is that he is "a man who reiterates his disdain for travel while he peppers his writings with its products; . . . a writer who urges his readers to concentrate upon a knowledge of their own local plot of ground while he makes sure in his writings that their acquaintance with the world is nothing less than global; . . . the seemingly contented provincial who is all the while devouring the accounts of other men's farthest travels" (p. 48). Thoreau was an avid reader of travel books, particularly those which dealt with the explorations of Canada and America, but he also read of the sea voyages of Darwin and Cook and of the explorations of South America, Asia, Africa, and the Arctic. A strong interest in travel gripped him, without question, but as he explained in his letter to Issac Hecker of 14 August 1844, it was an interest that remained subordinate to others. "Your method of travelling especially—to *live* along the road—citizens of the world, without haste or petty plans—I have often proposed this to my dreams and I still do—But the fact is, I cannot so decidedly postpone exploring the *Farther Indies*, which are to be reached you know by other routes and other methods of travel" (*Correspondence*, p. 156).

Even if Thoreau could be considered an armchair traveler, however, he could not upon that basis alone be classified as cosmopolitan. More germane to the proof of his qualities of cosmopolitanism would be an indication of those literary influences upon his work which show his readiness to borrow from foreign cultures. There were in fact several foreign sources from which he borrowed, but the first and possibly most profound from a literary point of view was the classics. He had been thoroughly grounded in the classics even before entering Harvard, and while he was a student there he undertook the customary classical studies, including Greek, Italian, and Latin, languages and literatures. His writings are filled with references to the classics, and a number of his contributions to the *Dial* were translations from or commentaries upon the classics, e.g., Aeschylus, Anacreon, Persius, and Pindar. Van Wyck Brooks called him "the best Greek scholar in Concord" (*The Flowering of New England*, p. 284, cited in Walter Harding's *Thoreau Handbook*, New York, 1959, p. 100), and Ethel Seybold amassed so much factual and logical proof of Thoreau's indebtedness to the classics that her thesis must be considered incontrovertible. She showed that the classical authors had been his models for imitation, materials for translation, and sources for many of his notions about language, government, history, poetry, and music. They proved to be not only a mine of information about another world but also "a kind of symbol of that world, an encouraging glimpse and a proof of the existence of a still greater and yet surely attainable world" (p. 85). More specifically she proved that in his youth Thoreau had read the epic writers, the dramatists, the lyrists, and the biographers; after *Walden* he turned to the husbandry writers; and finally he read the geographers, anthropologists, and naturalists.

By nature, however, Thoreau was a combination of antipodals, and classicism, deeply imbedded as it may have been in his mind, exerted no exclusive influence. To the basically romantic character of Thoreau the more recent literature of Europe—if not so remote in time or place as the classical, although quite properly remote for an American romanticist—had almost as strong an appeal. The breadth of his interests in European literature is borne out by his readings in Dante, Fenelon, Tasso, Goethe, La Fontaine, Schiller, Ariosto, Voltaire, and Zimmermann. He read French well, and some Italian, Spanish, and German. In a letter to his friend B. B. Wiley (26 April 1857), Thoreau recommended that Wiley read Gibbon, Franklin, Alfieri, Cellini, de Quincey, and Goethe (*Correspondence*, p. 478); and in his *A Week on the Concord and Merrimack Rivers* he included a tribute to Goethe (in *Writings*, I, 347-353). Thoreau had also read widely in Scandinavian literature. He read Linnaeus, Kalm, and Swedenborg, and he knew Norse history and mythology from the *Prose Edda, Heimskringla, Antiquitates Americanoe* of Rafn, and *Sagas of the Norse Kings* by Samuel Laing. His knowledge of English authors, a knowledge which extended even to such relatively unknown writers as Francis Quarles, was so evident that some scholars have concluded that his acquaintanceship with continental literature was of comparatively little importance. Even if this opinion were correct—it is being constantly revised by more recent scholarship—it would not exclude the possibility of Thoreau's cosmopolitanism. For in establishing the presence of cosmopolitan elements in Thoreau's works, the degree of influence of the several European literatures does not seem to be of such importance as the fact of their existence.

One of the primary connections between Thoreau and the cultures of the West and the East was the transcendental movement. Since its sources were German and it came to America principally through Coleridge and Carlyle, it had a strongly cosmopolitan cast to it; further, its chief organ, the *Dial*, was broadly international in scope. Besides the classical authors it included such important contemporaries or near contemporaries as Goethe, Schelling, Bettina Brentano, Jean Paul Richter, and Kant. In addition, this internationally oriented journal presented literature and commentary thereon from China, India, and New England. That Thoreau shared in this eclectic policy is evident in his thirty-one contributions.

For Thoreau as for the other transcendentalists, the line between religion and philosophy was seldom clear. To this difficulty was added the blatantly unorthodox and international quality of his belief. As a result, many of his contemporaries, in particular those with the narrowest convictions and deepest prejudices, were outraged by his paganism, as it was often termed in his time, or his pantheism, as it is more commonly termed today. His writings were filled with damning evidence. "In my Pantheon," he wrote in the *Week*, "Pan still reigns in pristine glory" (I, 65), But classical paganism was only one facet of his many-sided religion. "The reading which I love best is the scriptures of the several nations," he wrote in the *Week*, "though it happens that I am better acquainted with those of the Hindoos, the Chinese, and the Persians, than of the Hebrews" (I, 72). With his untranscendental belief in the existence of evil and his interest in Persian religion, a fair case could be made for him as a Zoroastrian (v. *Walden*, e.g., p. 185); yet in spite of his breadth of interest and in spite of his profession of ignorance of the scriptures of the Hebrews, the facts remain that his writings abounded with references to the Bible, and his familiarity with that book, notwithstanding his interest in a universal religion containing Christianity, surpassed that of certain of his contemporaries who publicly professed their Christian belief. Christianity to Thoreau was a sort of bed of Procrustes, and at best he rested uneasily upon it. Most students of Thoreau would agree that neither his religion nor his philosophy could be said to be subject to local narrow attachments and prejudices. There is simply too much in his writing which repudiates restrictive religion.

No remarks about Thoreau's religious and philosophical ideas would be complete without acknowledgment of the profound effect which the beliefs of the Orient had upon him. It was this influence which was largely responsible for the pardoxically international cast to the views of the man who had scarcely ever left Concord, and its scope and depth have been well charted. It can be traced back to 1841, when Thoreau began to read oriental works from Emerson's library. Although his interest in such literature had diminished considerably by 1855, the year in which he received a gift of forty-four books of oriental philosophy and literature from his friend Cholmondeley, it never really disappeared. Echoes of it are to be found up through the last of his writings. The influence of the mystics of the Orient upon both his ideas and their expression has been demonstrated by Helen Snyder in a dissertation (Heidelberg), and the presence of many oriental images and symbols in his works has been shown by Kurt Leidecker in an article called "That Sad Pagan Thoreau" (*Visva-Bharati Quarterly*, 1951, pp. 218–259). Arthur Christy's *The Orient in American Transcendentalism* (New York, 1932) proves the existence of Thoreau's great interest in Yoga, the *Vedas*, and Confucianism principally by reference to the *Journal*. Using the *Journal*, the *Correspondence*, and the major published writings of Thoreau, Sreekrishna Sarma revises some of Christy's conclusions in "A Short Study of the Oriental Influence upon Henry David Thoreau" (*Jahrbuch für Amerikastudien*, 1956, pp. 76–92) and at the same time presents conclusive proof of the part which oriental thought played in the development of Thoreau's ideas. Sarma quotes from the *Journal* (6 August 1841) such statements as "I cannot read a sentence in the book of the Hindoos without being elevated as upon the table lands of the Ghants. It has such a rhythm as the winds of the desert, such a tide as the Ganges, and seems as superior to criticism as the Himmaleh mounts," and "One wise sentence [from the Vedas] is worth the state of Massachusetts many times over" (II, 4). Sarma also showed that Thoreau was a yogi who followed the so-called path of knowledge or Jñāna-yoga. Finally Sarma adduced a close relationship between Thoreau's belief in the transmigration and rebirth of the soul and the Hinduistic and Buddhistic beliefs in these same phenomena and the Law of Compensation. Several of Thoreau's statements lend support to this doctrine, but one particular quotation from *Walden* seems indisputable. "They [the owls] are the spirits, the low spirits and melancholy forebodings, of fallen souls that once in human shape nightwalked the earth and did the deeds of darkness, now expiating their sins with their wailing hymns or threnodies in the scenery of their transgressions" (p. 197). Much more research has been done in the attempt to understand Thoreau's idealogical relationships with the Orient, and all of it supports, directly or indirectly, the thesis that Thoreau was eclectic, not only in his eagerness to borrow from various cultures, but also in his willingness to draw upon these divergent materials in order to further his constant effort at formulating and expressing his ideas on philosophy and religion. His drawing upon these materials from the Orient as well as from the ancient and modern classics of the West reveals him as a man of not just one time and place. His early debt to other cultures will perhaps eventually be paid off as they discover in him not only something unique and foreign but also, at the same time, a dim reflection of themselves.

A Hundred Years of *Walden*

William Condry

WILLIAM CONDRY was originally a teacher of French, but after a few years' teaching turned to a more enduring interest, natural history, and to professional writing. Besides many articles and broadcast scripts, he has written a book on Thoreau, and several others on natural history —*The Snowdonia National Park, Birds and Wild Africa, Exploring Wales,* and *Woodlands.* He is now warden of a nature reserve owned by the Royal Society for the Protection of Birds.

A HUNDRED YEARS OF *WALDEN*

I like what old Walt Whitman once said about Thoreau: "... my prejudices, if I may call them that, are all with Emerson; but Thoreau was a surprising fellow—he is not easily grasped—is elusive: yet he is one of the native forces—stands for a fact, for a movement, an upheaval ... he looms up bigger and bigger: his dying does not seem to have hurt him a bit: every year has added to his fame. One thing about Thoreau keeps him very near to me: I refer to his lawless-ness—his dissent—his going his absolute own road let hell blaze all it chooses."

Thoreau made merry with society in deadly earnest. In order to think, he did not retire to a library to pore over dry-as-dust systems. Instead he went and borrowed a friend's axe and built himself a shanty by a pond, where he could grow rows and rows of beans. And as he worked he chuckled to himself at the odd ideas about life which came to him out there in the robust air with the smell of the healthy earth about him. And when he sat down to write in the evening, all those odd thoughts came tumbling out to make the merry masterpiece called *Walden: or Life in the Woods*, published in 1854. The book was republished from time to time for the remainder of the century, enjoying a modest following of enthusiasts especially this side of the Atlantic. In Ireland, W. B. Yeats recalled how his father's reading of *Walden* to him inspired him from boyhood with a yearning to have a Walden of his own, and in after years, remembering this desire, he wrote "Innisfree," whose "nine bean rows" are a reminiscence of *Walden*.

In England, where George Eliot had years before reviewed *Walden* kindly in the *Westminster Gazette*, Robert Louis Stevenson saw fit in 1880 to assail the book in an ill-humoured essay whose sentiments he afterwards recanted, admitting that Thoreau was one of the inspirations of his life and writing. Perhaps this recantation a staggering notoriety. *Merrie England* (1893) sold two million copies (mostly at a penny each) by rising at the psychological moment on the wave of social and intellectual discontent that swept through the Nineties. Blatchford was to the fore in the open-air movement as well. His ideas reached ever wider audiences through his popular paper *The Clarion*. There sprang up *Clarion* discussion-groups, *Clarion* theatre-groups, and through *Clarion* cycling-clubs town-bound young workers on their new "safety bicycles" sought the open countryside at weekends. Blatchford began *Merrie England* with the injunction that if his readers first read *Walden* they would more easily understand his book, and thousands read and took to heart Thoreau's message.

The turn of the century was an exciting time when alongside America's *Walden* one could breathe in even more daring new ideas from Europe in the works of Nietzsche, Kropotkin, Bakunin and Tolstoy; and when little magazines and pamphlets vied with each other to put across their various revolutionary messages. There was *The Eagle and the Serpent*, nineteen issues of which were published in London between 1898 and 1902 and which "Dedicated to the Philosophy of Life Enunciated by Nietzsche, Emerson, Stirner, Thoreau and Goethe, Labours for the Recognition of New Ideals in Politics and Sociology, in Ethics and Philosophy, in Literature and Art." In Derby there was published *The Candlestick*, whose editor, W. L. Hare, went to prison in 1902 for refusing to pay taxes to support the Boer War; in this act he was inspired by Thoreau's example, who as he related in *Walden*, spent a night in jail for refusing to pay the taxes imposed by a government which sent escaped slaves back into slavery. To go to prison for a principle was an act typical of the age, and found an echo a little later in the martyrdoms of the suffragette movement, and the pacifist movement of the first World War.

But 1914–18 changed everything, suddenly completing the triumph of science and mechanics. Before then few cars stirred the dust of the country roads. Many villages were as remote as they had been in the eighteenth century. Rural Old England was still much as the New England of *Walden*: the townsman's dream of a Thoreau-style rustic retreat still seemed possible. But in the intensively organised and urbanised society of the post-war years, the ideal of the simple life waned. That the popularity of *Walden* did not wane with it was a measure of the book's depth. There was and is an enduring core of readers who love *Walden*, not as a book full of clever and quotable ideas, but as the superbly expressed utterance of a man concerned not with "isms" but with the search for individual integrity.

Among modern writers there have been many who, like H. M. Tomlinson, have loved Walden. But none perhaps have been quite as captivated as H. W. Nevinson who directed his long-lasting energies to the support of the oppressed on so many fronts such as Greece, Turkey, Ireland, South Africa, India and Russia, as well as England. Visiting America in 1920, Nevinson went to see those "quiet relics of Concord: the houses of Hawthorne and Emerson." Then he walked out to Walden Pond: "There I sat long, for there was the place I had wished to visit more than any other in America. It was there my friend Thoreau had lived, and there in loneliness had conceived the little book which to me is the most beautiful product that ever sprang from American soil, as he himself was the most beautiful and courageous nature."

Now in this centenary year we can ask: will *Walden* remain readable for a further hundred years? I think it will. As long as a love of the open-air, of natural beauty, of intellectual freedom and of the dignity of the individual endures, *Walden* will be cherished.

Perhaps the prophecy made by W. H. Hudson in 1917 on the occasion of the centenary of Thoreau's birth will prove right. Hudson wrote: "I have failed to find, in all the books and articles on Thoreau which I have read, a satisfying and adequate statement or exposition of the man and his true place in the world of mind and spirit. The reason of my failure, it might be said, is that I have put him too high, that my enthusiasm has spoilt my judgment. . . . Nevertheless, I will stick to my belief that when the bicentenary comes round and is celebrated by our descendants; when . . . are forgotten all those who anatomized Thoreau in order to trace his affinities and give him his true classification—now as a Gilbert White, now as a lesser Ralph Waldo Emerson, now as a Richard Jefferies, now as somebody else, he will be regarded as simply himself, as Thoreau, one without master or mate, who was ready to follow his own genius whithersoever it might lead him . . . and who was in the foremost ranks of the prophets."

Thoreau in France

Maurice Gonnaud and Micheline Flak

MAURICE J. GONNAUD is Professor of American Literature at the University of Lyon. His scholarly interests in American literature have resulted in works on various authors, including R. W. Emerson, upon whom he has published most extensively. Recently he has been a Visiting Professor at the University of North Carolina, and subsequently at the University of California at Davis.

MICHELINE FLAK discovered *Walden* when starting her career as a young English teacher. Greatly impressed, she got in touch with the Thoreau Society of America and was encouraged by them to spread a better knowledge of Thoreau in France, which she has been doing since then through talks and articles. (See *Europe*, Juillet-Aout 1967, Special Issue on Thoreau.) She has translated *Civil Disobedience* into French (J. J. Pauvert, edit. Paris, 1968). She is now working on "Les Sources Philosophiques de le Pensée de Thoreau." Miss Flak is General Secretary of Les Amis Français de Thoreau and part-time assistant professor at the Sorbonne.

THOREAU IN FRANCE

Of all the major writers of the American Renaissance, Henry David Thoreau remained until recently the least appreciated in France. It looked indeed as if the French had decided to meet his determination to ignore Europe by a corresponding disdain for his name and his work. Except in paperback editions imported from the United States for students reading American literature within set syllabi, *Walden* was not obtainable in France. Nor has there been in the past any of those flurries of enthusiasm which now and then mark the temporary convergence of an outstanding foreign mind with the needs or ideals of a generation. For most Frenchmen, Thoreau's work is like the unexplored continent which he evokes at the end of *Walden*, but the urge to embark on a voyage of discovery is sadly lacking.

However, this overall picture admits of significant exceptions. Ever since the end of the nineteenth century there have been those who have responded to the spell of Thoreau, and the record they have left is well worth looking into. Because it was at no time fashionable in France to quote from "Civil Disobedience" or "Life without Principle," their voices still ring with excitement. Earnestness and a sense of wonder at the treasures they are about to disclose are the hallmarks of their writings. They stand in marked contrast to a handful of French professors, most of them residents of the United States, who have approached Thoreau's work more coolly, though not unperceptively, in an effort to describe its originality and suggest the unique cultural context in which it developed. At times the two images overlap, or shade into each other, but the resulting impressions differ sharply: unmistakable evidence of the gap dividing professors from literary or non-academic circles in France.

Properly enough, the history of Thoreau's reception in this country begins with an article by Thérèse Bentzon in the *Revue des*

Deux-Mondes (15 September 1887). Under the deceptive label of "Le Naturalisme aux Etats-Unis," the author offers what she believes will act as a welcome corrective to the decadent excesses of the French naturalists: "Perhaps it would not be unprofitable to show our old France, so hard to amuse, so curious about pleasures occasionally refined to the point of over-sophistication, the kind of pastimes that satisfy a country less jaded, anxious above all to remain 'manly' [in English in the text], and carrying those aspirations into art itself."[1] Claiming the first rank for Thoreau in that school of "outdoor" writers, she proceeds to give a description of his personality and literary achievement. The article is based on Sanborn's biography, but it occasionally indulges in naïve chauvinism, as when Thérèse Bentzon ascribes some of Thoreau's most solid virtues—"an imperturbable common sense, an extreme candor, a gift for writing charming letters, and a certain parochial spirit"[2]—to his Anglo-Norman ancestry.

The artist in Thoreau, especially the poet, is analyzed more convincingly; she shows real insight when, referring to a piece published in the *Dial*, "Sympathy," she remarks: "In these verses, there is not the least trace of imitation of the author of 'Woodnotes' [Emerson]; rather they would reveal an intense familiarity with the literature of the time of Elizabeth and the Stuarts."[3] Among the prose works *Walden* is praised for the serene self-possession it reflects, as well as for the perfection of its style. Unfortunately, the author's Gallic bias breaks through again in her comments on *A Yankee in Canada*, which she views essentially as a pious tribute to the sturdi-

---

1. "Peut-être . . . n'est-il pas inutile de montrer à notre vieille France, si difficile à amuser, si curieuse de raffinements poussés parfois jusqu'à la chinoiserie, les passe-temps dont se contente un pays moins blasé, jaloux avant toutes choses de rester 'manly,' et qui transporte dans l'art même ce genre d'aspirations."
2. "un bons sens imperturbable, une extrême franchise, le don d'écrire des lettres charmantes, et un certain attachement au clocher . . ."
3. "Ces vers ne témoignent aucune imitation de l'auteur de 'Woodnotes,' mais révèleraient plutôt une étroite familiarité avec la littérature du temps d'Elizabeth et des Stuarts."

ness of the French race. And she characteristically concludes on a moral note, intended to castigate her own compatriots for their fecklessness: "No matter what season it is that inspires him, it should be recognized that no American naturalist has ever been guilty of softening the soul by making Nature the accomplice of his passions, the echo of his own sorrows, of his own complaints. . . . Thoreau and his brothers in spirit have neither crimes, nor sorrows nor blighted hopes to forget. They go straight to Nature in a joyous, innocent, almost childlike impulse, with which even the most unsophisticated can sympathize; and this is for every one a very good example."[4]

Despite her occasional felicities of perception, Thérèse Bentzon misses the truly vital element in Thoreau's work. But the next generation of literary critics was to move away from that provincial, slightly patronizing attitude and hail Thoreau as one of the authentic voices of world literature. Their public, however, amounted to no more than a curious elite, anxious to break across the narrowness of national standards at a time when traditions had the support of the leading periodicals.

As early as 1896, two newly-founded journals reproduced freely translated excerpts from Thoreau's writings. One of these journals was the *Magazine International*, sponsored by the "Société Internationale Artistique," and edited by a young man who was to become one of the major exponents of American literature in France, Léon Bazalgette. In previous issues, the *Magazine International* had published some of Whitman's poems, as well as Emerson's "The American Scholar." In July of 1896 some fragments from Thoreau's diary, dated between 1852 and 1860, appeared in a translation by

---

4. "Quelle que soit la saison qui les inspire, on doit le reconnaître, aucun des naturalistes américains n'a jamais eu ce tort d'amollir l'âme en faisant de la nature la complice de ses passions, l'écho de ses douleurs et de ses plaintes . . . Thoreau et ses émules n'ont ni crimes, ni douleurs, ni désenchantements à oublier. Ils vont droit à elle d'un élan joyeux, innocent, presque enfantin, auquel les plus simples peuvent s'associer et qui est pour tous d'un bon exemple."

I. Will. It is hard to imagine the reasons for the selection beyond a desire to do justice to the variety and desultoriness of Thoreau's entries. The first extract, dated March, 1856, is a comparison between the allurements of Concord and those of Paris; most of the others emphasize Thoreau's healthy response to nature. The same number of the *Magazine International* also contains a translation of the first part of the preface to the 1855 edition of *Leaves of Grass,* as if one of the editor's aims had been to provide his readers with cumulative evidence of the freshness and range of American literature.

Much in the same way, in its issue of 1 November, one of the most brilliant literary magazines of the late nineteenth and early twentieth centuries, the *Revue Blanche,* printed excerpts from "Civil Disobedience" with an interesting preface by the translator, A. Phélibé. While the information derives from Salt's biography, Phélibé presents his own synthetic view of Thoreau's personality; not only does he hint at a possibly strong influence of Thoreau on his older friend Emerson, but he places the Walden experiment in a context of lifelong challenge and re-evaluation: "As a matter of fact, the return to Nature as he understands it does not imply a corresponding regression of civilization towards savagery; he considers civilization as a real advance in man's condition, but he wants to demonstrate at what price this advantage is bought to-day, and to suggest that all the benefits of civilization could be secured without man having to suffer from its current faults."[5] This aspect of Thoreau's message was to be picked up again intermittently by French critics up to our own day, though never with far-reaching echoes with respect to the public.

Another little review, the *Renaissance Latine,* gave its readers samplings of Thoreau's masterpiece. In December, 1903, and January, 1904, the magazine ran excerpts from *Walden* with a militant

---

5. "A la vérité, le retour à la nature comme il l'entend n'implique pas un regrés correspondant de la civilisation vers la barbarie; il considère la civilisation comme un réel progrès dans la condition de l'homme, mais il veut montrer au prix de quel sacrifice cet avantage est aujourd'hui obtenu, et suggérer que l'on pourrait s'assurer tous les bénéfices de la civilisation sans pâtir de ses inconvénients actuels."

preface by Maurice Muret: "At the time when Thoreau was living, the world was not yet ready to understand his language. He spoke in the wilderness, or just about. But since his death he has made a magnificent comeback. Right under our eyes, his work is completing a triumphant world tour. It is being discussed in England, commented upon in Germany. It was becoming urgent that it be known in France."[6] In fewer than thirty-five pages, three chapters of *Walden*, "Economy" (untitled in French), "Solitude," and "Reading," were skimmed so as to offer a dramatically shortened version of Thoreau's book. The translator was the Princesse de Polignac, an American by birth, who signed her maiden name, Winaretta Singer. But in the aristocratic coterie, to whose tastes the *Renaissance Latine* catered, Thoreau's political and social theories could hardly be appreciated; as Maurice Muret put it, somewhat complacently, at the end of his preface, "Questionable or worse than that when he addresses himself to major philosopohical, social or political topics, H. D. Thoreau meets with universal approval when he limits himself to recommending a return to nature. Voltaire once wrote to Rousseau: 'You make me want to get down on all fours.' The hermit of *Walden* deserves the same compliment."[7] A neat line was being drawn between the nature lover, or the artist, and the subversive thinker.

Failing to reach the wide audience that other European countries were already supplying, Thoreau remained in France for most of the first two decades of the twentieth century essentially a writer's writer, highly esteemed for his power over words and his bold plunges into man's inner spirit. Marcel Proust discovered him either through

6. "A l'époque où vivait Thoreau, le monde n'était pas mûr encore pour comprendre son langage. Il parla dans le désert ou à peu près. Mais il a pris depuis sa mort une éclatante revanche. Son oeuvre accomplit sous nos yeux un tour du monde triomphal. Elle est discutée en Angleterre, elle est commentée en Allemagne. Il devenait urgent qu'elle fût connue en France."
7. "Suspect, plus que suspect, lorsqu'il aborde les grands sujets philosophiques, sociaux, politiques, Henry David Thoreau rallie tous les suffrages quand il se borne à préconiser le retour à la nature. Voltaire écrivait à Rousseau: 'Vous me donnez envie de marcher à quatre pattes.' L'ermite de Walden mérite le même . . . compliment."

the *Revue Blanche,* which had published some of his own pieces in 1893, or, more probably, through the milieu associated with the *Renaissance Latine*, since he was on friendly terms with both the Princesse de Polignac and the editor of the review, Constantin de Brancovan, a brother to the Comtesse de Noailles. In his recent biography of Proust, George D. Painter alludes to Proust's disappointment when he heard that the Princesse de Polignac "had just completed a French rendering of Thoreau's *Walden*, which he and Antoine [Bibesco] had planned to translate together in the early days of their friendship." Indeed, one of Proust's letters addressed to the Comtesse de Noailles (15 January 1904) urges his correspondent with characteristic playfulness to read the Princesse's translation: "Read in the perfidious Latin Inconstancy, in the ungrateful Latin Vainglory, in the shocking Latin Impropriety [mock descriptions of the *Renaissance Latine*], which is nevertheless the best written review in Paris, the wonderful pages from *Walden*. It feels as though you were reading them out of your own soul, so strong is the sense that they issue from the very depths of one's innermost experience."[8]

No more shall be heard of Thoreau in Proust's work, but it may be, as Joel Porte hints in his recent book, *Emerson and Thoreau, Transcendentals in Conflict*, that Proust did learn something from Thoreau's impeccable grasp of concrete realities. It is also Painter's opinion, expressed in a letter to Mrs. Renée Lemaître (28 April 1967) that chapter three of *Walden*, "Reading," as translated by the Princesse de Polignac, influenced Proust's own essay on the same theme.

Another memorable tribute to the greatness of *Walden* came many years later from André Gide, in a special number of *Fontaine* (June-July, 1943) which was dedicated to the "Ecrivains et Poètes des Etats-Unis d'Amérique." When Gide was asked whether American

---

8. "Lisez dans la perfide Inconstance latine, dans l'ingrate Jactance latine, dans la choquante Inconvenance latine, qui est malgré cela la revue la mieux faite de Paris, les pages admirables de Walden. Il semble qu'on les lise en soi-même tant elles sortent du fond de notre expérience intime."

literature had meant a great deal to him, he replied that he had been one of the first Frenchmen to admire Melville, long before *Moby Dick* had been translated by Giono, and went on: "The same is true of Thoreau's *Walden*. I remember the day when Fabulet ran into me at the Place de la Madeleine and told me of his discovery: 'An extraordinary book, that no one knows about yet. . . .' Well, that book I had that very day in my pocket."[9] The year was 1913, and the friend met by chance on the street was the future translator of *Walden*. Again, it is tempting to speculate on possible influences, but the little episode recorded here took place no less than fifteen or sixteen years after the publication of *Les Nourritures Terrestres*, undoubtedly the book in which Gide's inspiration came closest to Thoreau's unique blending of mysticism and sensuous enjoyment. It would seem, rather, that the two writers, who shared in a common religious background (Gide had been born and brought up in a French Protestant family), rebelled with comparable violence against the deadening weight of tradition and transferred, in the process, huge inherited supplies of moral energy onto the plane of individual self-fulfillment.

Interestingly enough, Gide's meeting with Fabulet heralds a new period in the record—the only one, in fact, during which the personality and writings of Thoreau aroused a sustained interest in France and reached something like recognition. Within the next decade two of his books were translated, and a biography followed almost immediately. Reviews in various periodicals testified to a new awareness on the part of the reading public, and duly registered conflicting opinions. At long last, Thoreau seemed to be growing into a living force.

The first call to attention was sounded in the *Mercure de France*, an influential journal which for many years paid close attention to American literature, and fulfilled to some extent the part played in

---

9. "De même pour le *Walden* de Thoreau: je me souviens du jour où Fabulet rencontré place de la Madeleine, me fit part de sa découverte: 'Un livre extraordinaire! que personne encore ne connaît. . . .' Ce livre, je l'avais, ce jour-là, dans ma poche."

the nineteenth century by the *Revue des Deux-Mondes*. In a well-informed, well-thought-out article, "La Littérature Américaine," published in the issue of 16 January 1919, Vincent O'Sullivan lodged a plea for two masterpieces unjustly ignored by the French public—*The Scarlet Letter* and *Walden*. About the latter he commented further: "In the same way, *Walden*, by H. D. Thoreau, could not have been written anywhere else than in America. Thoreau was entirely original, much more so than Emerson, with whom he is sometimes very stupidly associated. If his prose and poetry could be translated into French as competently as Whitman's works, he would be admired by the same European public to which Whitman appeals."[10] Two months later, another token of Thoreau's art was given to the French public when Philéas Lebesgue translated a letter dated 26 September 1859 for the *Cahiers Idéalistes Français*.

However, in spite of O'Sullivan's insistent praise, *Walden* was not the first of Thoreau's books to reach the shelves of French booksellers in translation. In 1921, Léon Bazalgette, who in the meantime had devoted himself to spreading the fame of Whitman in France, brought out a miscellany of pieces under the general title of *Désobéir*. The book contained seven items, covering the whole span of the author's literary career, arranged roughly in a descending scale of aggressiveness: "La Vie sans Principe" ("Life without Principle"); "Désobéir aux Lois" ("Civil Disobedience"); "L'Esclavage chez nous" ("Slavery in Massachusetts"); "Pour John Brown" ("Plea for Captain John Brown"); "Ses derniers Moments" ("Last Days of John Brown"); "Marcher" ("Walking"); "L'Hôte" (dated 1843 by Bazalgette). In a foreword, Bazalgette described his book as an extension of *Walden*, designed to suggest the real stature of Thoreau. Beyond the expert in natural history, beyond the artist, he extolled the untamable libertarian, who had shed all illusions about

---

10. "*Walden*, de H. D. Thoreau, n'a pu lui aussi naître qu'en Amérique. Thoreau fut parfaitement original, autrement plus original qu'Emerson auquel on le rattache parfois bien stupidement, et si l'on traduisait sa prose et sa poésie en français aussi bien qu'on a traduit l'oeuvre de Whitman, il aurait du succès auprès de ce même public européen à qui Whitman plaît."

the common run of men and could yet appeal untiringly to man's inner nobility: "He demanded of his neighbor, in order to be able to call him brother, that he possess certain essential qualities; if he were lacking in those, he was no longer a man in the estimation of Thoreau, who would then riddle him with taunts, hoping secretly all along that he would arouse the pride of the sleeper—that failure, that caricature, that traitor to humanity."[11]

If some of the reviewers were only lukewarm in their praise, Bazalgette's book sparked off Romain Rolland's enthusiasm. In an unpublished letter to Mme Cruppi of 17 December 1921 (quoted here through the courtesy of Mme Romain Rolland), the great humanitarian writer cried out his admiration: "Do you know Thoreau (an American and a contemporary of Whitman)? Bazalgette has just published at Rieder's a French translation of one of his volumes called *Civil Disobedience*. It is a superb book. It should be the Bible of every strong conscience that refuses to obey the State's unjust demands."[12] The next day, in another unpublished letter (to Lucien Price; again quoted through the courtesy of Mme Rolland), he rounded off his estimation of Thoreau's importance to us: "What a magnificent fellow! And how up-to-date he still is! Some of his writings, *Civil Disobedience, A Plea for Captain John Brown*, could be used in today's struggles. They should be the Bible of Individualism with a capital I."[13] Later, in his biography of Vivekananda (*La Vie de Vivekananda et l'Evangile Universel*, 1929) Romain Rol-

---

11 "Il exigeait de son prochain, pour pouvoir l'appeler son frère, qu'il possédât certaines qualités essentielles; sinon ce n'était plus un homme à ses yeux et il le criblait de brocards—non sans le secret espoir d'éveiller l'amour-propre de l'endormi, ce raté, cette caricature, ce crime de lèse-humanité."

12. "Connaissez-vous Thoreau (l'Américain, contemporain de Whitman)? Bazalgette vient d'éditer en traduction française, chez Rieder, un volume de lui intitulé *Désobéir*. C'este superbe. Ce devrait être la bible de toutes les consciences fortes, qui refusent d'obéir aux injustices de l'Etat."

13. "Quel magnifique bonhomme! Et comme il est encore actuel! Certains de ses écrits, *Désobéir aux Lois, Plaidoyer pour John Brown*, etc. . . . pourraient être utilisés dans les luttes d'aujourd'hui. Ce devrait être la Bible du grand Individualisme."

land briefly described the group at Concord, and Thoreau received his due measure of attention for his pioneering interest in the literature of India. Among French writers of the first magnitude, he may be said to have been the only one to have responded fully to the two crucial strains of Thoreau's philosophical message: his recognition of a mystical unity in the world, and his call to resist the encroachments of organized political powers.

A year after Bazalgette's *Désobéir*, Louis Fabulet's translation of *Walden*, with its meaningful alternative title, *La Vie dans les Bois*, duly emphasized, came out in Paris. It had been for the translator a labor of love which had occupied seven years of his life. In a substantial preface, Fabulet explained how Thoreau's tutelary spirit had guided him through the hardships and miseries of the first World War to a reassessment of man's fundamental values; the passage deserves to be quoted at some length because it reveals in its author the exact blending of the moralist, the visionary, and the artist which *Walden* seemed to have been written to captivate:

> It is not today that I feel in the heart of darkness. It was in 1913, on the eve of the War. I had asked Rudyard Kipling to restore some red blood to French veins. I was asking Walt Whitman to define for France the goal for which she was too often blindly fighting, that is to say for Love, Cosmic Love, Omnipotent Love. I had gone to Francis of Assisi to ask him to relieve me of all that I felt was weighing me down, and that was nothing more than a myriad of artificial needs created by a civilization based only on material possessions and designed to suppress all human beauty. And I felt myself coming as if by a natural drift to Henry Thoreau, who I later learned passes for the American St. Francis, the St. Francis of our time. How can I describe my rapture at discovering in Thoreau, precisely and succinctly stated, the final thoughts to which I had been led by a sustained intellectual effort ever since the day when I had begun to think as a man. And the glorious end to which they pointed was a state of happiness which every single word of *Walden* triumphantly embodied.[14]

14. "Ce n'est pas aujourd'hui que je me sens au fond des ténèbres. C'était en 1913, à la veille de la Guerre. J'avais demandé à Rudyard Kipling de

The translation itself was more than competent; with occasional purple patches, and a fastidiousness of language verging on preciosity, it fairly reflected Thoreau's paradoxical turn of mind as well as his meticulous craftmanship. The book was well received, and, almost immediately, ran through several editions (the copy available to readers at the Bibliotheque Nationale dates from the seventh). One of the best reviews, signed J. A. (Jane Alexandre), appeared in *Libres Propos*, a little journal edited by Alain, himself an intractable opponent of political tyranny (one of his books is called, in Thoreauvian manner, "Le Citoyen contre les Pouvoirs"). Jane Alexandre viewed Thoreau as a kind of literary Cézanne, in love with the physical fullness of the world, but aware of the artist's mission, which is to break up the shapes of things so as to fashion them anew and turn them into imperishable objects of beauty. She also pointed to the Adamic purpose of the Walden experiment, carried out by a man intent on becoming "that wild creature dazzled by the face of the world like the first man on the first day."[15] Her conclusion was that Thoreau had won for himself the dignity of fellow-traveller to men of all ages.

In February, 1923, a new periodical, *Europe*, was launched with a view to fostering a more generous international spirit in a continent still aching from the woes of the war. Romain Rolland had

---

remettre du sang rouge dans les veines françaises. Je demandais à Walt Whitman de préciser à la France le but pour lequel trop souvent en aveugle elle combattait, c'est-à-dire l'Amour, l'Amour Cosmique, l'Amour omnipotent. J'étais allé à François d'Assise pour lui demander de me débarrasser de tout ce que je sentais m'encombrer, et qui n'était que les mille besoins artificiels multipliés par une civilisation ne reposant que sur la matière, pour l'étouffement de toute beauté humaine. Et j'arrivai comme naturellement à Henry David Thoreau, que j'appris plus tard passer pour le François d'Assise de l'Amérique, le François d'Assise de nos jours. Dirai-je mon ravissement à trouver ici précisées, résumées, les pensées finales auxquelles tout le travail de ma pensée depuis l'âge où l'homme commence à penser m'avait amené? Et pour quelle fin! Pour un bonheur dont il n'était pas un mot de *Walden* qui ne fût la réalisation triomphante."
15. "ce sauvage ébloui par la face du monde comme le premier homme au premier jour."

been one of the leading spirits in the enterprise, and Léon Bazalgette, the one-time editor of the *Magazine International*, was not long in joining the team. In the number dated 15 May 1924, Bazalgette gave, quite cryptically, an extract of his forthcoming biography of Thoreau under the title "La Bonne Fortune"; about the same period, the book itself was announced in a blurb which, beyond the expected boosting-up of its excellence, endeavored to establish an interesting literary parentage: "It is a work dedicated to the glory of the whole, free, indomitable man, who makes light equally of wealth and of the direst poverty, of hypocritical constitutions and of hypocritical honors. If a book similar in spirit to this one must be cited, I will choose Jules Vallès's. Since the publication of *Jacques Vingtras*, there has not been in our literature a work of that caliber, nor one that is capable to the same extent of creating a broad movement of ideas."[16] Jules Vallès (little remembered today) had been actively involved in the political battles of his day unlike Thoreau who, for most of his life at least, had been unwilling to jeopardize his independence and to join in the fray; but both writers had poured themselves out into their books, and—more important still—had drawn, each in his own way, the profile of the modern insurgent.

It is not necessary to comment in detail on Bazalgette's treatment of Thoreau's life, since there is an English version of his book by Van Wyck Brooks, also published in 1924 (it may not be irrelevant to recall here that Van Wyck Brooks shrank from a literal translation of the title, *Henry Thoreau Sauvage*, and substituted instead a phrase from Emerson). Bazalgette's work is anything but scholarly in the austere, painstaking sense of the word. In his survey of the criticism devoted to Thoreau, Lewis Leary has called the book "a dramatized biography in the manner of André Maurois," and the

16. "C'est une oeuvre écrite à la gloire de l'homme intégral, libre, irréductible, qui se rit de l'argent comme de la misère, des hypocrites constitutions commes des hypocrites honneurs. S'il faut choisir un parrain à ce livre, choisissons Jules Vallès. Depuis *Jacques Vingtras*, notre littérature n'a pas vu naître d'ouvrage de cette classe, ni susceptible, autant que celui-ci, de déterminer un grand mouvement d'idées. . . ."

contemporary reader feels inclined to support this estimate; indeed he must every now and again suppress a twinge of annoyance at Bazalgette's high-handed narrative technique. But one should bear in mind that this measures the shift in scholarly standards since the 1920's, rather than Bazalgette's own achievement. The book, now long out of print, remains a valuable landmark; it mirrors the mood of part at least of a generation, and substantiates a then popular conception of literary biography. Nor should one forget the high esteem in which Bazalgette was held by French and American writers alike. When he died in 1929, *Europe* prepared a special number (15 June 1929) to pay homage to his work as pioneer of American letters in France; from among the batch of messages sent in for the occasion by various American authors, that by Dos Passos deserves best to be retrieved: "Bazalgette," he wrote, "was one of those Frenchmen who really knew America. Through Whitman and Thoreau, he was introduced to an America incomparably bigger and more essential than the country of jazz, skyscrapers and Negro joints so much in vogue in the France of today. There is the magnificent weightiness and tangible solidity of earth about his book on Thoreau."[17] Thus for a brief moment had the pulse of the socially-minded, leftist, French intelligentsia, and that of some of the leading figures of the Lost Generation throbbed in unison.

In its issue of 15 December 1924, *Europe* harbored yet another piece of Thoreauvian literature, a long fragment from *A Week on the Concord and Merrimack Rivers* introduced and translated by Louis Fabulet. The twenty-odd pages, excerpted from chapter VI, "Wednesday," were presented as an essay on Friendship, which to all intents and purposes they were, since they represent Thoreau's

17. "Bazalgette," he wrote, "fut l'un des Français qui connurent le mieux l'Amérique. Par Whitman et Thoreau, il a connu une Amérique autrement vaste et plus fondamentale que ce pays de jazz, de gratte-ciel et de bouis-bouis nègres, si fort à la mode en France de nos jours. Son livre sur Thoreau est une oeuvre qui a la magnifique gravité, le grain dru de la terre." The English version in the text may not be altogether literal because it is taken from a French translation of the original, now unobtainable, letter which Dos Passos wrote in English.

most detailed treatment of the subject. Fabulet did not balk at rating Thoreau's idea of friendship higher even than that of Montaigne; only the New Englander had dared to insist on its divine nature and refused to have it tarnished by sentimental attachments; once again, he was being held up to the readers' admiration as an immensely wise, if exacting, model.

Fabulet and Bazalgette stand somewhat apart in the small phalanx of French critics because of an unflagging earnestness in their vindication of a man whom they honored as something more than an artist in words. After their withdrawal from the literary scene, a certain militant tone, akin to that of the convert or the proselyte, was not heard again, at least in literary circles. By contrast, the criticism of the late 1920's bears the stamp of the new academic spirit, made up of caution and sympathy, honestly committed to its subject, imaginative when at its best, but eschewing the rhetoric of faith.

Two names here immediately come to mind: those of Andrée Bruel and Régis Michaud. Andrée Bruel, born and brought up in France, taught French literature at Wellesley College for over thirty years. Interested from the outset in the literature of the country in which she had elected to live, she published, in 1929, her doctoral dissertation, *Emerson et Thoreau*, a delicate record of the friendship which had developed between the two major figures of the Transcendentalist movement, as well as a perceptive analysis of their basic attitudes as writers. The book has stood the test of time well; in his already quoted *Emerson and Thoreau, Transcendentalists in Conflict*, Joel Porte departs from some of its interpretations, but graciously acknowledges his debt to the clear-mindedness and sound scholarship of its author.

Régis Michaud is another Frenchman who spent most of his life in the United States, teaching in various universities between 1907 and 1939. His first book, *Mystiques et Réalistes Anglo-Saxons* (1918) had failed to distinguish between English and American writers; along with those of Emerson, Whitman, Twain, London, he had surveyed the works of Walter Pater and Bernard Shaw, as well as those of two notable expatriates, Henry James and Edith Wharton. Gradually, however, he had come to focus his attention on what he judged to be typical of America's literary personality. In a book published in 1924, *La Pensée Américaine: autour d'Emerson*, he had devoted a whole chapter to Thoreau, stressing the aesthetic originality of the author of *Walden*, and placing him on a par with such famous European literary figures as Blake, Wordsworth, Ruskin, and Pater. But it was not until 1930 that he saw fit to supplement the work of Bazalgette and Fabulet by translating, with the assistance of S. David, large extracts from Thoreau's diary under the title *Un philosophe dans les Bois (Journal de Thoreau)*. In fact, he did not limit himself to the material announced in the title; by way of a preface he printed Emerson's famous essay on Thoreau and followed up the extracts from the diary with two pieces illustrative of his full maturity, "Ktaadn, récit d'une excursion," and "Les Appels de l'Ouest, éloge de la vie sauvage," which is Michaud's own rendering of "Walking."

Michaud's response to Thoreau is anything but obtuse. In a fine introduction he expressed his preference for the *Journals* rather than for *A Week* or even for *Walden*, because in the *Journals* the reader was confronted with a man in his most natural state, innocent of the ambition of tidying up his style. Commenting on Thoreau's fierce individualism, he pointed to its historical roots in Puritanism and went on to describe with remarkable acumen the novelty and ambiguity of his stance in front of Nature: "Through sheer renunciation and deliberate poverty, he had attained supreme perfection, the Buddhist beatitude of the Yoga. He had wedded so completely his soul and his senses that he had reached a crystalline state of innocence, vision, and absolute purity in his perceptions, a sort of mystical sensualism, in which the exceptional sharpness of the senses was attended by a truly orgiastic ecstasy."[18] Michaud's book is not

18. "A force de dépouillement, de renoncement, il était arrivé à la perfection suprême, à la béatitude bouddhiste du Yoga. Il avait si bien marié l'âme aux sens qu'il avait atteint à un état cristallin d'innocence, de clairvoyance et de pureté totale de ses perceptions, une sorte de sensualisme

unworthy of Bazalgette's *Désobéir*, but clearly an ideal of fidelity to historical truth, of cultured comprehension, had been substituted for the rich glow of enthusiasm which had suffused the earlier volume.

By 1930, academic criticism had taken over almost absolutely. Pierre Brodin's *Les Maîtres de la Littérature Américaine* (1946), in which Thoreau's literary stature is recognized unequivocally, Cyrille Arnavon's *Histoire Littéraire des Etats-Unis* (1953), with its brief, but penetrating treatment of the man and his work, were paramount in shaping, for a steadily increasing public of university students, a literary figure closely patterned upon the findings of recent American scholarship. But no French "thèse" making Thoreau its central concern has yet been published; nor has there been any attempt, since the end of World War II, to add a significant contribution to the wealth of critical literature lavished on him, year after year, across the Atlantic. It would seem that French scholars, in that particular field, confined their ambitions to a correct appraisal of the work done elsewhere.

Perhaps the only milieu in which the Thoreauvian leaven is still active is the little known, though by no means clandestine, world of die-hard libertarians. For them, Thoreau is a heroic figure, and they like to remind themselves of their debt to him in their little magazines. In 1959, one of their most respected leaders, E. Armand, gathered a sheaf of articles on Thoreau in a special number of *L'Unique*, a monthly bulletin published as a supplement to *Défense de l'Homme*. Under the title, "Thoreau, ce qu'il fut et ce qu'on en a dit," ("Thoreau, what he was and what has been said about him") Armand himself introduced the subject, recalling with fervid eloquence his life-long admiration for Thoreau, and exalting the lesson of the indomitable rebel: ". . . Thoreau was not only a man returned to a state of wildness (only relatively speaking of course), he was a non-conformist, an outsider, an anarchist, scornful of the values which the Americans of his day (at least a large number of them)

---

mystique où la suracuité des sens se double d'un véritable transport orgiaque."

thought important. An implacable foe of militarism and slavery alike, an earnest advocate of non-violent resistance, rejecting political action as well as the complexities of society, condemning superfluous and useless objects as detrimental to the moral well-being of the individual, this is how Thoreau appears to us in his writings and his actions."[19]

As might be expected, the tenor of this issue is touchingly uneven. One of the articles reconstructs freely the history of social and economic systems so as to credit Thoreau with insights which a more strict chronology would have denied him. Another one coins with superb assurance the word "naturianisme" to define the modern solution, admirably adumbrated by Thoreau, to the conflict between society and solitude, but fails to carry the philosophical attempt any further. On the other hand, some of the contributions are of a fine intellectual calibre, especially an essay by Benjamin de Casséres, which had already appeared, in a translation by Armand, in another anarchistic journal, *L'En-Dehors*, in March, 1929. For de Casséres, Thoreau is the man who learned to expect nothing of life, and succeeded proportionately in making his life worth living: "The soul expects the great Event, the great Romance—the Unique Adventure —which never occurs. The soul has missed the Event because it was expecting it. Thoreau was not expecting anything. Here and Now were for him the Great Event. Life itself was for him the unique adventure."[20] It would be tempting to push de Casséres' idea a

---

19. ". . . Thoreau ne fut pas seulement l'homme redevenu 'sauvage' (bien entendu très relativement), c'était un non-conformiste, un 'en-dehors', un an-archiste, un contempteur des valeurs auxquelles les Américains de son temps attachaient de l'importance, un grand nombre d'entre eux en tous cas. Adversaire acharné du militarisme comme de l'esclavagisme, propagandiste de la résistance passive, réfractaire à l'action politique comme à la complication sociétaire, jugeant le superflu et l'inutile comme portant atteinte à la santé morale de la personne humaine—tel nous apparaît Thoreau dans ses écrits et dans ses actes. . . ."
20. "L'âme attend le grand Evénement, le grand Roman—l'Unique Aventure—qui n'arrive jamais. Elle l'a manqué parce qu'elle l'attendait; Thoreau n'attendait rien. Ici et maintenant était pour lui le Grand Evénement. La vie était pour lui l'unique aventure."

little further, and to describe Thoreau as the exact opposite of John Marcher, Henry James's sorrowful hero in *The Beast in the Jungle*.

Such, approximately, is the record of Thoreau's reception in France until a very recent past. None too comforting, one will have to admit. Thoreau was "discovered" rather late, and Thérèse Bentzon's article in the *Revue des Deux-Mondes* inaugurated a tradition of misunderstanding or, to say the least, of dubious understanding. For one thing, the originality of American literature was not fully realized by French critics until the third decade of this century, and Thoreau suffered, like many others, from being approached in a spirit both patronizing and embarrassingly naïve. Maurice Muret's sweeping judgment, in the *Renaissance Latine*, on Thoreau's ineptness as a social thinker, as well as his smug praise of the disciple of Rousseau, are more than individual reactions. At the turn of the century, the French were still unable, on the whole, to cast off national and social prejudices, and to admit not only that perhaps nature meant something else besides walking on all fours, but that foreign writers ought to be measured by their own yardsticks. Because he was the paramount example in French-Swiss literature of a studied dedication to nature, Jean-Jacques Rousseau was used over and over again as an exclusive reference, and allowed to dictate the law in a realm which tolerates, and indeed invites, the recognition of cultural differences.

It may be also that the French are at heart a political nation, with but little confidence in, and enthusiasm for, the curative virtues of wild nature. This writer must confess that the provocation inherent in Leon Bazalgette's title, "Henry Thoreau sauvage," strikes him as slightly awkward; a "sauvage" is not an ideal to be upheld convincingly in front of a Frenchman, if only because the word is associated ever since his childhood with brutal connotations. Significantly, even the ugliness of the first World War failed to alter this disposition appreciably. Reviewing in February 1922 Bazalgette's *Désobéir* for the *Nouvelle Revue Française*, Benjamin Crémieux praised the healthy vigor of the book, but dismissed Thoreau's political philosophy as super-annuated, irrelevant to France's post-war conditions: "Intellectually and morally, it would seem difficult for Thoreau to exert a great influence. Had he been translated before the war, things might have been different. But after five years spent in the mud of the trenches or in the woods, the Western man seeks happiness not in a return to primitive life, but in a more rational and equitable management of civilization. When someone today is unhappy with the political regime, he becomes not an anarchist but a communist. He does not try to escape social restraints, but to modify the way in which they affect us; and in doing so, he accentuates rather than relaxes their pressure."[21] Perhaps one might contend that in a country as thoroughly fashioned by the spirit of Catholicism as France is, any doctrine ultimately derived from a Protestant ethic, in its insistence on the unlimited rights of the individual, was bound to find a majority of the reading public skeptical and potentially hostile. Except for a small fringe of self-styled "outsiders," Thoreau has always been, and is likely to remain, an eccentric figure, to be taken with a grain of salt.

Still, signs of a long-delayed recognition seem to be looming on the horizon. In October, 1966, at the instigation of Mr. Leonard Kleinfeld, a branch of the Society of the Friends of Henry Thoreau was set up in France with the active support of university professors and lycée teachers. The year before, in March, 1965, the secretary of the Society, Miss Micheline Flak, had given a lecture, "Henry David Thoreau ou l'Homme Révolté," for the members of the "Foyer Individualiste," one of those lay conventicles in which the fire of spiritual rebellion is kept burning. Published as a pamphlet by the "Ruche Ouvrière" press, it may be taken as a symbol of the

---

21. "Intellectuellement et moralement, il me semble difficile que Thoreau puisse exercer une grande influence. Traduit avant la guerre, il aurait pu n'en être pas de même. Mais après cinq ans de tranchées et de vie dans les bois, ce n'est pas le bonheur par la suppression de la civilisation que cherche l'Occidental, mais par un aménagement plus rationnel et plus équitable de la civilisation. Quand on n'est pas content du régime aujourd'hui, on ne devient pas anarchiste, mais communiste. On ne cherche pas à s'évader de la contrainte sociale, mais à en modifier les conditions, sans la relâcher, bien au contraire en l'accentuant."

existence, henceforth, of a common ground for admirers of Thoreau from all walks of life. Finally, in the last few months, Pierre Abraham and Pierre Gamarra, the editors of *Europe*, the periodical which had done so much to spread Thoreau's fame in the 1920's, decided to acknowledge the 150th anniversary of his birth by a series of critical contributions on a scale unprecedented in France. Nearly half the pages of the issue for July-August, 1967 are devoted to Thoreau, the other half going to monthly chronicles and to a parallel homage to the great Swiss novelist Ramuz, not unlike Thoreau in his deep-seated love for his native "canton."

Aiming at a public of interested, but relatively uninformed readers, the editors have met their problem wisely and skillfully. The general transcendentalist background is conjured up by Micheline Flak in "L'homme de Concord," while a selective bibliography and a chronological table of contemporary events, both of them prepared by Laurence Vernet, provide the necessary bearings. Micheline Flak contributes another richly documented article, "Thoreau et les Français," which has been drawn on so heavily and so unashamedly for this report that it has seemed that the only way to recognize the debt at all adequately, was to put both names under it, in open coauthorship. The progress of Thoreauvian scholarship is reflected in two estimates by Roger Asselineau, professor at the Sorbonne, and Jean Normand, professor at the University of Rennes. In "Un Narcisse Puritain," Professor Asselineau takes a rather acid view of his subject, and points to the crippling effect of the contradictions under which Thoreau labored; because "this naturalist who was also a lover of natural forms distrusted nature,"[22] he ended up fabricating his *Journal* instead of living his life. Professor Normand's article, "Les Ironies de la Solitude," is a brilliantly written piece on Hawthorne and Thoreau. In both cases, the authors search well below the surface of facts for an explanation of Thoreau's puzzling identity, and they find it in a rich complex of national and individual traits. Another significant contribution, illustrative of a method

---

22. "ce naturaliste doublé d'un naturiste se méfiait de la nature"

much in favor today, is J. P. Raudnitz's "Thoreau ou l'humus retrouvé," in which the fundamental link between man's soul and some of nature's obscure forces is explored; an interesting comparison is made in passing with the work of a nineteenth century French poet, Maurice de Guérin.

Nor is Thoreau the uncompromising individualist neglected in this issue. An old admirer of Bazalgette's books, Louis Simon, charts the course of political rebellion from Thoreau's days to our own in an article whose title, "De Désobéir au Crime d'Obéir," suggests two of the author's gospels of independence (*Le Crime d'Obéir* is the title of a novel published about 1895 by Han Ryner, an out-and-out spiritual insurgent who gathered a small following of disciples and, though long since dead, continues to be honored in a periodical publication, *Les Cahiers des Amis de Han Ryner*).

The rest of the pages devoted to Thoreau are filled by translations, and again the balance is nicely kept between academic and non-academic writers. The latter are represented by Henry Miller's preface to *Life Without Principle* published in 1946, and reprinted in 1962 in a collection of essays, *Stand Still Like the Humming-Bird*; the former by Walter Harding, whose speech at Washington and Concord in 1962, on the occasion of the celebration of the 100th anniversary of Thoreau's death, is reproduced under the title, "L'Influence de la Désobéissance Civile." Properly and modestly, Thoreau himself brings up the rear with well-chosen extracts from his writings.

After this account of what undoubtedly amounts to an important literary event, it would be wrong to assign Thoreau to a French limbo of forgotten, or wanly remembered, shades. Something has happened to his fame already, and more is coming, since two new translations are due; the first one, by Germaine Landré, will be a fresh rendering of *Walden*, to be published by Aubier, a firm specializing in bilingual editions; the other, sponsored by Jean-Jacques Pauvert, well-known for his bold and seldom unsuccessful publishing ventures, will contain under the same cover "Civil Disobedience," translated by Micheline Flak, and "A Plea for Captain John

Brown," translated by Christine Demorel and Laurence Vernet. Perhaps, after all, Thoreau's day is only beginning to dawn in this country. Perhaps what we had taken for the timid sun of his reputation, at the time when Bazalgette and Fabulet were striving to propagate his name, was only a morning star.

Postscript (December 1970)

Since the completion of this chapter, the interest in Thoreau in France, on a markedly upward trend over the last five years, has in no way abated. Reprints of Fabulet's translation of *Walden* and Michaud's collection of extracts from the *Journal* came out in 1967; both volumes are already out of print. Further translations of Thoreau's works have been announced by French publishers as due in a few months. Weekly or monthly periodicals have continued to pay attention to the challenging and startlingly relevant doctrines of the hermit of *Walden*:

> Raymond Las Vergnas, "Le Triomphe de Thoreau," *Les Nouvelles Littéraires*, 26 February 1968.
>
> Micheline Flak, "Thoreau le Désobéissant," *Planète*, May-June 1968.
>
> "Actualité du philosophe H. D. Thoreau," *Humanisme*, March-April 1969.

Finally, several doctoral dissertations by well-informed and imaginative scholars are by now well under way.

Thoreau and Van Eeden

Seymour L. Flaxman

SEYMOUR L. FLAXMAN, born in 1918, is Professor of German at The City College of The City University of New York. He is also Executive Officer of the Program in Germanic Languages and Literatures at the Graduate Center CUNY, and is a member of the doctoral faculty in Comparative Literature there. Professor Flaxman is the author of *Herman Heijermans and His Dramas* (The Hague, 1954) and editor of the newsletter *Neerlandica Americana*.

THOREAU AND VAN EEDEN

The man who admitted only that he had "travelled a good deal in Concord" never set foot in the Netherlands. Yet Thoreau's ideas crossed the Atlantic, and had a great influence there. For many years *Walden* was a word in daily use in the Netherlands and it appeared frequently in the press, although it did not always have the meaning Thoreau had given it.

Thoreau's influence and reputation in Holland are mainly due to the work of Frederik van Eeden (1860–1932), one of the most striking figures in modern Dutch literature. Van Eeden is usually associated with the Dutch literary movement known as "de Beweging van Tachtig," or the Movement of Eighty.[1] In the Eighties a group of young Dutchmen, Kloos, van Eeden, Verwey, Paap, and van der Goes, launched a literary revolution that was destined to overthrow the artificial rhyming and fossilized sentiments—van Eeden satirized both very cleverly—of the older generation. *De Gids* (*The Guide*), the leading literary periodical in the Netherlands, was to them the symbol of outworn tradition. In opposition they set up *De Nieuwe Gids*, which was to be a new guide for a new lit-

---

This article is the outgrowth of a paper originally read before the Comparative Literature Section of the Ninth University of Kentucky Foreign Language Conference at Lexington, Kentucky, on 27 April 1956. It was then revised and expanded for publication in *Der Friede: Idee und Verwirklichung: The Search for Peace. Festgabe für Adolf Leschnitzer*. (Heidelberg: Lambert Schneider, 1961), 341–352. There has been some further revision for publication here. I should like to express my thanks to Professor W. Gs Hellinga of the University of Amsterdam and to the Universiteitsbibliotheek for their kindness in microfilming certain materials for me.

1. G. Stuiveling has defined van Eeden as a member of the *Nieuwe Gids* group, rather than of the Beweging van Tachtig; cf. "Frederik van Eeden Tachtiger of Nieuwe Gidser," *Mededelingen van het Frederik van Eeden Genootschap*, III (1936), 6–16, republished in *Rekenschap* (Amsterdam, 1947), 201–27.

erary generation. This was the beginning of the modern period in Dutch literature.

Actually de Beweging van Tachtig, or "de Nieuwe Gidsbeweging," as it was often called, was not a well-organized school, but only a loose association without a unified program. No common aim or widely shared belief held this group of individualists together, and once they had successfully challenged the authority of the older generation and cleared the way for young writers, they nullified the cohesive force that bound them together, and each went his separate way. Verwey, in 1889, was the first to leave the movement, and by 1893 Kloos was alone at *De Nieuwe Gids*.

The divergence in the two main literary influences on this group indicates the diversity of their views. Van Deyssel, a prose writer, was a great admirer of Zola and an enthusiastic supporter of Naturalism, although he wanted an independent and truly national art. On the other hand, it is not difficult to detect the strains of Romanticism or the influence of Keats and Shelley in the poetry of the Nieuwe Gidsers, and the men of the *Nieuwe Gids* achieved their best results in the field of poetry. The effective word and the well-chosen simile were of the first importance to them, and they added new power and meaning to the Dutch language. But they also encouraged introspection and the highly subjective examination of emotion, and they worshipped beauty. The lyric and the sonnet were their favorite forms.

Frederik van Eeden was one of this group, and along with Kloos, he was an editor of *De Nieuwe Gids*. Yet he had been interested in literature long before he came under the influence of the Movement of the Eighties, and even if he had not joined it as one of its leaders, he would still be an unusual and interesting figure.

Van Eeden is one of those extraordinary physicians, who, like Schiller, Chekhov, and Schnitzler, appear with such striking frequency in literary history, and leave their mark there, rather than in the annals of medicine. Sometimes, like van Eeden, they are men of no little scientific talent. Thus, there are two great influences on van

Eeden's intellectual life. His father was a botanist, and as a boy, Frederik van Eeden had an attic room that was fitted out for the study of zoology. He planned to study medicine, but even at the age of fifteen he showed literary talent, and attempted to write verse.

In 1879 he went off to the University of Amsterdam to study medicine, but before he received his degree, he had already acquired a literary reputation. His first published work, *Het Rijk der Wijzen* (*The Realm of the Sages*), appeared anonymously in 1881. When this poetic drama was received with praise, however, he regretted not having signed his name to it. During his next years as a student, he wrote five more plays, *Het Sonnet, Frans Hals, Het Poortje* (*The Little Gate*), *De Student thuis* (*The Student at Home*), and *Don Torribio*, and he was moved by the emotions of ambition and success. He helped found *De Nieuwe Gids*, and his novel *De Kleine Johannes* (*Little Johannes*) was printed serially in its first issues in 1885.

At the end of this novel Johannes resolves to "become a good man." This resolution symbolizes the social idealism that was to play such an important part not only in the whole Nieuwe Gids Movement, but in van Eeden's life as well. Van Eeden was influenced by German Romanticism, but there are Romantic characteristics in his personality as well as in his literary style, as is evident from his interest in spiritualism, the occult, and parapsychology.

In Paris, where he spent some time studying medicine, van Eeden became interested in psychiatry and parapsychology, and was particularly impressed with Charcot's experiments in hypnotism. He received his degree from the University of Amsterdam in 1886, a few months after his marriage. Then he settled in Bussum, a little town about fifteen miles from Amsterdam, and there set up his practice. Hardly a year had passed before he grew bored, and he decided to visit the town of Goes, for a friend had told him how Dr. van Renterghem was treating his patients there by hypnosis. Van Eeden was so enthusiastic about what he saw in Goes, that two weeks later he suggested to van Renterghem that they establish a clinic for hypnotic therapy in Amsterdam. This became the first psychiatric clinic in the Netherlands, and it brought both men fame and financial rewards.

Van Eeden's literary reputation, meanwhile, continued to grow, not so much because of the lyrics inspired by his love for Ellen, perhaps, but because of the novel *Johannes Viator* (1892), a continuation of *De Kleine Johannes*, and the dramas *De Broeders* (*The Brothers*), written in 1894, and *Lioba* (1896).

Meanwhile, van Eeden began to drift away from the Movement of the Eighties. His article "Verstand en Gevoel in de sociale Evolutie" (Reason and Feeling in Social Evolution), which was published in *De Nieuwe Gids*,[2] revealed an important intellectual current that was to move not only van Eeden, but several others out of the sphere of influence that radiated from this magazine. At the same time, it indicated the course van Eeden was to follow.

As an important industrial center, with thousands of diamond workers, Amsterdam was a natural focus for the rising Socialist movement. It was here, in the seventies and eighties, that Dutch Socialism began, and in the late eighties and nineties, there were strikes in the city. Some of the individualists at the *Nieuwe Gids*, like Kloos, were unmoved by these events, but others, like van der Goes, devoted themselves to the realization of social ideals. Thus arose an irreparable breach that split *De Nieuwe Gids* itself. Van Eeden decided that he was a socialist by feeling (as opposed to a theoretical socialist, who had arrived at his position by reason), and he turned to social reform and social experiment.

As early as 8 May 1897 he had visited an agricultural colony, De Batelaar, and in June he was inspired by the sight of a colony of huts in the Vierhoutensch Woods.[3] ". . . I now have only *one*

---

2. Frederik van Eeden, "Verstand en gevoel in de sociale evolutie," *De Nieuwe Gids*, V (1890), 377–388. He had read widely in the social theorists; cf. Frederik van Eeden, *Happy Humanity* (New York, 1912), 117–119.
3. Albert Verwey, *Frederick van Eeden* (Santpoort, 1939), 144. For an account of van Eeden's life see also G. Kalff, Jr., *Frederik van Eeden: Psychologie van den Tachtigers* (The Hague, 1927).

ideal," he wrote in his diary, "to live my life in such a hut, in that woods."[4]

Yet the greatest inspiration for his attempt to realize his social ideals came not from his Dutch or European contemporaries, but from an American transcendentalist who had died almost forty years before. Thoreau had not been completely unknown in the Netherlands. Potgieter, a member of the generation that had dominated Dutch literature in the middle of the nineteenth century, possessed several of his works.[5] But these were all in English, for Thoreau had not been translated into Dutch. Van Eeden also read him in English, and *Walden* made a tremendous impression on him. On 24 January 1898 he confessed to his diary, "I am reading Thoreau. A strong Thoreau atmosphere prevails. We are talking about colonies that we will establish, and I am searching constantly for suitable places for a hut or little house."[6]

Van Eeden soon made plans for a little hut to be covered with straw, and after living in this for a while, he decided that there ought to be more than one hut. On 24 April 1898 van Eeden bought the Cruysbergen estate between Bussum and 's-Graveland. He also persuaded a wealthy young woman to buy an estate adjacent to his.[7] In 1899 he started a cooperative colony, which he named Walden. But as he said later, this "only proved that I admired Thoreau as an author, not that I shared all his views."[8] As a matter of fact, van Eeden not only did not share Thoreau's dislike of machinery, but he believed that modern industrial and administrative methods would lead to the success of his cooperative community. It is also rather amusing to read van Suchtelen's account of *de Lelie*, van

---

4. *Ibid.*
5. R. Pennink, "Potgieter en de Amerikaanse letterkunde," *De Nieuwe Taalgids*, XXXIII (1929), 273–294.
6. Verwey, *op. cit.*, 144. Van Eeden read a borrowed copy of the Riverside Edition; cf. Lewis Leary, "Walden Goes Wandering: The Transit of Good Intentions," *The New England Quarterly*, XXXII (1959), 7.
7. C. W. Bieling, "Frederik van Eeden's Walden," *The Thoreau Society Bulletin*, XIV (January 1946), 1–2.
8. Frederik van Eeden, "Some Experience with People," *The Independent*, LXIV (1908), 446.

Eeden's own home at Walden, with its "warm luxury, which he, as a reformer, had to deny, but which was so entirely, so essentially a part of his innermost being as an artist and a man of the world."[9]

He had worked happily in his little hut, writing *Van de koele meren des doods* (*The Cool Seas of Death*), a novel portraying the psychological disintegration of a young woman. Van Eeden even thought he would like to be buried beside his hut.[10] Perhaps it was his great mistake, therefore, that instead of being content with the lonely kind of independence that Thoreau had sought, he planned a vast social experiment, in which large numbers of people would work for the common benefit. Believing that one ought to practice what one preached, he gave all the money derived from his literary work, about $600 a year, to the support of the colony. In order to promote the activities of the colony, he also gave lectures and tried to obtain financial contributions. But practical difficulties soon arose, As he admitted several years later:

> The greatest difficulty against which I had to struggle was the flocking in of people who were unsuited and unwanted. An investigation like the one intended can not take place in secret, and curious and indiscreet persons, journalists and sensation-hunters flooded the land and spread the wildest and most mendacious gossip. The result was that serious and sound workers kept aloof, but anyone who was at all inclined to be eccentric or who felt himself out of place in ordinary life came to Walden.
>
> Society is full of lost souls and failures who are searching for escape and rescue. And as soon as they heard anything about a "new society," they came to obtrude themselves as the most suitable and desirable.[11]

For such workers the name Walden soon became a mocking acros-

---

9. Nico van Suchtelen, "Muziek op Walden," *Mededelingen van het Frederik van Eeden Genootschap*, VII (1940) 62–63.
10. *Brieven van Frederik van Eeden: Fragmenten eener brief-wisseling uit de jaren 1889–1899* (Amsterdam and Leipzig, 1907).
11. Frederik van Eeden, "De Vrije Arbeid op Walden," *Studies*, Vijfde Reeks (Amsterdam, 1908), 62.

tic: "Waar Allen Luieren Daar Eet Niemand/Nochthans Eet Die Luiert Als Wij (Where All Laze Doth Eat None/Nevertheless Eat Doth he who Lazes As We)."[12]

Van Eeden aimed at a kind of Christian Socialism, in contrast with Marxian Socialism, which attracted some of the other members of the Nieuwe Gids Movement. Herman Heijermans, whose plays reflected his commitment to Socialism, attacked van Eeden's brand of socialism in *De Jonge Gids*.[13]

The colonists were expected to lead a simple life and to work for low wages. Most families had a house of their own, but paid no rent. If a colonist left, however, he had to leave his house and land, without attempting to sell them.[14] "From the very first," he admitted later, "I wanted to find the practicable form of social organization that would *spread*. I did not aim at all the personal satisfaction of living in secluded and cloisterlike happiness and purity."[15] He hoped to build a number of similar colonies and to join them all together. For this purpose he founded the Vereeniging Gemeenschappelijk Grondbezit (The Society for Community Ownership of the Land) in 1902.

A sister colony had been established at Blaricum, for example, but the land was poor, and the colonists had no knowledge of agriculture. It was a Spartan life, carried out on a vegetarian diet. Both the men and the women wore work clothes, and the men did not shave. Communal life and the question of admitting new colonists created difficulties. By the spring of 1902, however, there were asparagus beds, fruit trees, and a printing plant.[16]

12. *Ibid.*, 63.
13. Herman Heijermans, Jr., *De Jonge Gids*, II (1899), 817–827. This article also indicates the shock which van Eeden's words had on the middle-class audience that had paid to hear his lectures. For them, Heijermans says, van Eeden turned out to be "a Trojan horse." (817).
14. J. van Hettinga Tromp, "Van Eeden en 'Walden'," *Mededelingen van het Frederik van Eeden Genootschap*, III (1936), 31.
15. Frederik van Eeden, *The Independent*, LXIV (1908), 447.
16. A. Perdeck, "De Ramp van Blaricum," *Mededelingen van het Frederik van Eeden Genootschap*, III (1936), 23.

There were some twenty colonies of the Society for Community Ownership of the Land, spread all over the Netherlands, but "of all these groups Walden was the oldest, the largest, and the most prosperous."[17] None of the original "kindred spirits" was left, and conditions had improved. A bakery, started in 1902, prospered. Its whole wheat bread won a good reputation; it was soon sold in the village, and then throughout the country. There was also a poultry farm, and a plant for the preparation and packaging of cocoa. Honey was another product, for van Eeden was a skilled apiarist.[18] When van Eeden had collected the workers he could count on, he formed the Vereeniging Walden (The Walden Association), which was legally incorporated in 1903. He bought a sixty-acre farm a few miles away, with the idea of turning it into a dairy farm.

Yet, in the end, it was the Society for Community Ownership of the Land, as well as van Eeden's devotion to other social problems that proved the downfall of Walden. The colony named in honor of Thoreau might still be flourishing in Bussum today, now a suburb of what might be called Greater Amsterdam, had not a series of other social calamities forced its destruction.

In 1903 there was a big railroad strike in the Netherlands, and van Eeden championed the workers. At Blaricum the Catholic and Orthodox Protestant neighbors stormed the colony, tried to set the buildings on fire, and smashed the houses. The colony was soon abandoned.[19]

The strike failed, however, and the workers were locked out. In order to aid them, van Eeden began to collect a subscription fund. Contributors received stamps, which could later be turned in for merchandise. The plan met with enormous success, and in less than a year there were 40,000 contributors and more than $1,500 a week in contributions. The second year there were 70,000 contributors, but the weekly income, unfortunately, did not increase at the same

17. Frederik van Eeden, *Studies*, Vijfde Reeks, 54.
18. C. W. Bieling, *loc. cit.*
19. A. Perdeck, *op cit.*, 24–25.

rate. There were now four shops in Amsterdam, two in The Hague and Rotterdam, and agencies all over the country, selling furniture, manufactured goods, fuel, earthenware, shoes, kerosene, etc. The loss on all these operations was reduced to $6,000, compared with $12,-000 at the end of the first year.

Van Eeden demanded that his workers submit to strict business rule, or he would abandon them. They agreed, and he put the whole matter into the hands of a young friend, who persuaded him to leave and return to his literary work. "I only too readily complied," said van Eeden later, "went to Germany and wrote what I think to be a very good drama. But this drama cost me $100,000."[20]

The play was apparently *De Zendeling* (*The Missionary*), which was completed at the end of December 1905 and reflects the events of the railroad strike. Van Eeden had drawn great encouragement from his talks with Kahane, the *Dramaturg* of the Deutsches Theater in Berlin. He was filled with great hopes, which were eventually to end in disillusionment, for neither Kahane nor the Dutch theatrical companies would undertake a production of *De Zendeling*.

The $100,000 van Eeden referred to represents the sum of the indebtedness arising out of the bankruptcy of his vast subscription enterprise, de Eendracht (Unity). This bankruptcy involved not only generous relatives, but the 70,000 little contributors, for whom he felt personally responsible. Van Eeden exhausted his personal fortune to pay these debts, and was also left with a heavy burden of financial obligations.

Although the bakery and the truck farms had made the colony self-supporting, things now began to go badly at Walden. It finally became clear to everyone that a manager was needed. Van Eeden gave the colonists the choice of accepting a manager or leaving the colony. This time his strategy failed. Most of the workers chose to leave. They even started a competing organization in the immediate neighborhood, taking the customers with them. Van Eeden, with no workers to run the dairy farm, the truck gardens, or the bakery,

20. Frederik van Eeden, *The Independent*, LXIV (1908), 450.

and with new electrical equipment that had just been purchased now lying idle before him, was left to his fate.

Eventually Walden was reorganized with new workers, but all van Eeden's property was sold at public auction to satisfy the creditors in the bankruptcy proceedings, and as he later put it, he was forced to take up a "new Bohemian career."[21]

His Bohemian wanderings took him to the United States in 1908, and he arrived in New York on the *Mauretania* on February 28. The League for Political Education had invited him to come. He wrote a number of articles for the *Independent*[22] and the *World's Work*, describing his experiences at Walden and expounding his solution for the problems of modern society. He also described his medical experiences with psychology and psychiatry. He returned in the fall to lecture, appearing before the Civic Forum in New York. Charles Evans Hughes, then Governor of the State of New York, William Jennings Bryan, and Edwin Markham had also appeared before the Forum, among whose Vice Presidents were William Howard Taft, Samuel Gompers, and Bryan.

"In the first place," he told his audience, "my experience taught me in a decisive way that our original form of Communism as practised by the ancient Christians, according to the Gospel, is not only utterly impossible, but also undesirable."[23]

Although he was disillusioned, he believed that his experiment had been worthwhile. To the readers of *The Independent*, he admitted:

21. *Ibid.*, 451
22. Frederik van Eeden, *The Independent*, LXIV (1908), 443–451; "Impressions of America," *Ibid.*, LXV (1908), 370–374; "One More Cooperative Effort," *Ibid.*, LXVII (1909), 319–320. Cf. "The Visit of van Eeden," *Current Literature*, XLIV (1908), 292-294, M. Irwin Macdonald, "Frederik van Eeden: Poet, Novelist and Practical Communist," *The Craftsman*, XIV (1908), 127–136; Frederik van Eeden, "How Mind Can Heal the Body: A Record of Personal Experiences and Observations," *The American Magazine*, LXVI (September 1908), 531–539; "Curing by Suggestion," *World's Work*, XIX (September 1909), 11993–11999; "Happy Humanity," *Ibid.* (February 1910), 12588–12594, (March 1919), 12658–12661.
23. Frederik van Eeden, *Practical Communism—Work and Bread*, published as No. 6 of the Civic Forum Addresses (New York, 1908), 9.

I readily agree that seen in the light of history, my undertaking had all the appearance of a very foolish, naïve and clumsy one. Yet I must do myself justice once more. I know perfectly well the history of the different attempts of the same kind in America and elsewhere. The harm done to me by those ever-preached and never-practised Christian doctrines went not so deep as it did in that venerable but misguided prophet Tolstoy. I never was a Tolstoyan, how often people may have called me so. Nor was I a Ruskinian, how great my admiration for that splendid genius might be. I did not believe in non-resistance, nor did I reject the aid of machinery in the struggle for existence. And the name "Walden," given to my settlement, only proved that I admired Thoreau as an author, not that I shared all his views.[24]

Then in a spirit very much like Thoreau's, he goes on to state:

I believe I am justified in saying that I have by no means occasion to be proud of my blunders; neither have I reason to be ashamed of them, as I sacrificed whatever I had for the benefit of my country and the common good. Tho the details of my experiment are morally extremely painful, the whole effect on me is no worse than that of a private excursion to some unknown country or to the North Pole, a thing which surely costs not less, and leaves not more tangible results.[25]

Van Eeden visited President Theodore Roosevelt in Washington. He found him a man of action, not a philosopher. He was a strong man, conscious of his power. He also met Taft in Washington, and discussed his colonization plans with him.

In 1909 an article in *The Independent* described plans to set up a cooperative colony on a tract of 11,000 acres near Wilmington, North Carolina.[26] A prospectus, *Van Eeden-Kolonie In N. Carolina, U.S.A.*, appeared in Amsterdam in 1912.[27] Written in Dutch, but partly translated into bad English, it contained a letter from van Eeden offering advice to the colonists.

24. Frederik van Eeden, *The Independent*, LXIV (1908), 446.
25. *Ibid.*, 451
26. Frederik van Eeden, *The Independent*, LXVII (1909), 319–320.
27. This book also bears the title *Van Eeden-Colony in N. Carolina U. S. A.; Information for Settlers with a Letter by Dr. Frederik van Eeden.*

Be on your guard against fanatics and zealots, they have always spoiled the best schemes. Allow access to your community in a large, broad-minded way. Your strength will increase with your number and your principle is universal and invincible. In fact, to work for each other, workers for workers, and to get rich in a honest way, are devices that no sane human being can oppose. Nothing more is wanted as the binding idea of your community. In all other respects you may allow full freedom of opinion.[28]

The colonists were to purchase their land from the North Carolina Truck Company, and van Eeden and a certain Hoggson proposed the Co-productive Company. One of the colonists testified that "a very nice house can be built for two hundred to two hundred and fifty dollars."[29] The Atlantic Coast Line had built a Van Eeden Station near the colony, and Thoreau is mentioned in the prospectus.[30]

By the end of World War II this colony had disappeared, but not without creating benefits for the State of North Carolina, including a flower-growing industry worth three million dollars a year. But van Eeden was a writer, and the importance of his social experiments lies not so much in their practical success, but in their literary significance. Van Eeden drew other writers to Walden. Thus he invited Henri Borel (1869–1933) to visit him, assuring Borel that he would not have to live on a vegeterian diet.[31] Borel did not accept this invitation until more than half a year later, in May 1905, but he later described this as "the most beautiful period of my whole life."[32]

Adriaan van Oordt (1865–1910) joined van Eeden at Walden, and van Eeden wrote the introduction to his first novel, *Irmenlo*. Van Oordt later turned against van Eeden's theories, but van Eeden continued to admire his literary ability.

Of even more importance to Dutch literature than Borel and van

---

28. *Ibid.*, 75.
29. *Ibid.*, 30.
30. *Ibid.*, 51.
31. *Brieven van Frederik van Eeden aan Henri Borel* (Den Haag-Brussel, 1933), 128.
32. *Ibid.*, 130.

Oordt was Nico (Nicolaas Johannes) van Suchtelen (1878–1949), who spent the years 1898–1900 at Walden. *Quia Absurdum* (1906) reflects his experiences at the colony.

The first Dutch translation of Thoreau's *Walden*, with a foreword by van Eeden, appeared in 1902.[33] In September of the same year van Eeden wrote

> This book will disappoint many. I know that it is being looked to as one of the books that can guide us in the search for the New Life. But it will not be what most expect. There is none of that leading, enthusiastic, exciting, more or less passionate quality that most of the searching ones among us desire. They will find the book vague, disjointed, without foundation or wisdom.
>
> Yet there is more natural wisdom in this book than in many books that are considered sound scholarship. With a few sentences he shows that he has a much higher and deeper intellect than men who, in our time, pass for "powerful thinkers." In all the subtlety and erudition of Marx, for example, there is none of that broad and clear insight that Thoreau has when he expresses himself now and then with a single word that he has loosely tossed out.
>
> Thoreau is of the race of Carlyle, Emerson, Walt Whitman, Ruskin, and Tolstoi. Men of strong character, vigorous language, broad general wisdom, and what is the main thing—independence. They do not immerse themselves in economic speculation, but with their clear intellects easily see through the follies of the economists who fancy themselves wise. . . .
>
> Thoreau's great importance comes from his courage and his independence. He feels deeply, and dares to express straightforwardly what he really feels. He is like a tree that has grown straight among millions of stunted growths. In a normal society he would not be anything special, but in our society, where almost all suffer from a moral deformity, he has acquired the significance of a genius and a prophet.[34]

---

33. Henry D. Thoreau, *Walden*. Met een voorwoord van Fred. van Eeden en een inleiding van W. H. Dircks. Uit het Amerikaansch vert. door Suse de Jongh van Damwoude (Bussum, 1902).
34. Frederik van Eeden, *Studies*, Vierde Reeks (Amsterdam, 1904), 396–397.

On the other hand, van Eeden's *Van de koele meren des doods* was translated into English as *The Deeps of Deliverance* and published in New York and London in 1902.[35] *De Kleine Johannes* appeared as *The Quest* in Boston in 1907[36] and in New York and London in 1911.[37] *Ysbrand* was performed at the University of Kansas, and a translation, "with photographs of the author and the orignal American cast," was published there in 1910.[38] *De blijde wereld*, the group of lectures he had given in Holland to support his Walden experiment, was translated for publication in New York as *Happy Humanity* in 1912.[39] *De Nachtbruid*, a novel, appeared in an English version, *The Bride of Dreams*, in New York and London the following year.[40]

The failure of his Walden experiment did not, of course, put an end to van Eeden's literary career. He began work on a trilogy, *Sirius en Siderius* in 1909, and published the first part, *De ouders* (*The Parents*), in 1912, the second part, *Het Kind* (*The Child*), in 1914 and the last part, *Geroepen of Verkooren* (*Called or Chosen*), in 1924. The death of his son Paul reflected in *Pauls Ontwaken* (*Paul's Awakening*), which appeared in 1913. One of his best plays, *De Heks van Haarlem* (*The Witch of Harlem*) was published two years later.

The events of the Walden years found their way into the plays that followed *De Zendeling*, and they were transmuted into the action of *Minnestral, Ijsbrand, De Idealisten of Het beloofde land*

---

35. Frederik van Eeden, *The Deeps of Deliverance*. Tr. by Margaret Robinson, with an introduction by Will H. Dircks (New York and London, 1902).
36. Frederik van Eeden, *The Quest*. Authorized translation by L. W. C[ole] (Boston, 1907).
37. Frederik van Eeden, *The Quest*. Translation from the Dutch by Laura Ward Cole (New York—London, 1911).
38. Frederik van Eeden, *Ysbrand: A Tragicomedy*. Authorized translation. With photographs of the author and the original American cast. (Lawrence, Kansas, 1910).
39. Frederik van Eeden, *Happy Humanity* (New York, 1912).
40. Frederik van Eeden, *The Bride of Dreams*. Authorized translation by Mellie van Auw (New York and London, 1913).

(*The Idealists or the Promised Land*), *'t Paleis van Circe* (*Circe's Palace*), and *In Kenterend Getij* (*In the Turning of the Tide*) which, although it was not published until 1913, contains the earlier drama *De Zendeling* and *De Stamhouder* (*The Son and Heir*).

Verwey, who wrote a somewhat disenchanted study of van Eeden, included the novels *De Nachtbruid* and *Sirius en Siderius* with this group of plays, asserting that in each work van Eeden was portraying the noble hero in conflict with society. According to Verwey, van Eeden always saw himself as the noble hero, who was martyred by society.[41] In the foreword to *De Idealisten*, on the other hand, van Eeden scoffed at the idea of identifying him in his heroes.[42] But how can the reader help being reminded of van Eeden's own experience by such lines as these from *De Idealisten*?

> Call me a fool, who let himself be taken in
> by sly knaves and unworthy fellows;
> I'd rather go the way of such fools
> than that of the wise,
> who do not risk their honor
> and stand safe from scorn and mockery.
> The Promised Land lay farther than I thought.[43]

It is not only the influence of Thoreau on van Eeden and, through him, on other Dutch writers that is important, for van Eeden's reputation extended far beyond the Netherlands. He was also an international literary figure, and the pages of *Liber Amicorum*, the testimonial volume presented to him by his friends on his seventieth birthday, show the range and variety of his literary friendships.[14] There are tributes from his Dutch friends, like Nico van Suchtelen, of course, but there are also the praises of Hermann Bahr, Martin

---

41. Albert Verwey, *op. cit.*, 199 ff.
42. Frederik van Eeden, *De Idealisten* (Amsterdam, 1909), 5–7.
43. *Ibid.*, 176: noem mij een dwaas, die zich bedriegen liet, / door slimme boeven onwaard'ge lieden, / den weg van zulke dwazen ga ik liever / dan dien der wijzen, die hun eer niet wagen / en veilig staan voor smaad, en spotternij / 't Beloofde Land lag verder dan ik dacht.
44. *Liber Amicorum* (Amsterdam, 1930). There is a picture of van Eeden before his hut in Walden facing p. 181.

Buber, Sigmund Freud, Sir Oliver Lodge, Romain Rolland, Upton Sinclair, Felix Timmermans, Stefan Zweig, and Rabindranath Tagore, whose poetry he had translated into Dutch.

More significant than the question of influence, perhaps, is the process by which the work and fame of an author spread beyond his native land. There is something fascinating about the metamorphosis of Thoreau's *Walden* into van Eeden's experiment in "internal colonization" and its reimportation into the United States through the visiting Dutch lecturer.

Thoreau's Critical Reception in Germany

Eugene F. Timpe

THOREAU'S CRITICAL RECEPTION IN GERMANY

After Thoreau got back the unsold copies of his *A Week on the Concord and Merrimack Rivers* he wrote, "I have now a library of nearly nine hundred volumes, over seven hundred of which I wrote myself" (*Journal*, 28 October 1853). Even more than his own admission, an abundance of evidence which is gradually accumulating shows that during his own lifetime he had little success in disseminating either his books or his ideas. But this same body of information points to the fact that during the twentieth century his words and ideas have found increasing acceptance, not only in America but elsewhere. It is common knowledge that Gandhi was indebted to "Civil Disobedience" for the techniques of passive resistance which he used to such good effect in South Africa and India, it is known that while under German occupation during the second World War the Danes successfully employed a form of passive resistance which had been inspired by Thoreau, and it is a matter of record that a group of Dutchmen once actually established a colony modeled in part upon *Walden.* No such dramatic actualizations of Thoreau's ideas took place in Germany; yet his reception in that country was substantial, occasionally even vigorous, and a description of it establishes another segment of that total pattern which can help us to see to what extent and in what ways his ideas found their way abroad.

From even a cursory inspection of the main features of Thoreau's reception in Germany it becomes evident that unlike Longfellow's or Cooper's or Harte's it followed no particular pattern. It actually took place during two separate periods. The first began about 1890 —until thirty years after his death he was almost totally ignored, even by such collectors of minutiae as nineteenth-century literary historians—and ended around 1910. This was his primary period in Germany. Nearly a dozen articles of a scholarly nature, two of which were of some importance, apparently created sufficient interest so that three publishers offered translations of *Walden* and one of the selection from his Journal called "Winter." The first of these, which was also the first translation of *Walden* into a foreign language, made its appearance in 1897. It was issued in two further editions and one additional printing during the next seven years, and imitation of it in a new translation by the well-known firm of Diederichs leaves little doubt that publication of Thoreau was at that time an attractive business venture, even though a lapse of seventeen years between the first and second editions of the Diederichs book suggests that the success of this undertaking was greatest during the relatively short first period of interest in Henry David Thoreau.

Between the two wars Thoreau was almost completely neglected in Germany, but during the Americanization era following the second World War, his writings, like those of other American authors, enjoyed increasing popularity. His revival—there were four new translations during the first five years after the war and these were quickly followed by a number of dissertations—was initiated apparently by publishers evincing a sensitivity to the demand for things American rather than by academicians.

A closer look at the subject reveals some of its details. Apparently Thoreau was first noticed in Germany in 1867, the year in which the competent but anonymous author of the general article on American literature in the Brockhaus encyclopedia (*Allgemeine deutsche Real-Encyklopädie für die gebildeten Stande Conversations-Lexikon*, 11th edition, Leipzig, 1864–68) described Thoreau as one "who with tender thoughtfulness brings to nature a noble human awareness and a microscopic sharpness of observation" (X, 840). None of the several nineteenth-century histories of American literature even mentioned Thoreau until Rudolph Doehm, in his *Aus dem amerikanischen Dichterwald* (Leipzig, 1881), wrote a paragraph on Thoreau which contained as its principal remark the statement that Thoreau had deferred to his brother when it turned out that they both loved the same young lady. Even Eduard Engel's *Die amerikanische Litteratur*, although it dealt generously with such literary celebrities as Dorgon, Osgood, Wetherall, Tourgee, Cable, Habberton, and Halleck, did not even mention Thoreau's name until the fourth edition (Leipzig, 1897), in which Thoreau was described as an American Rousseau and a political nihilist.

The change of fortunes came in 1891, and the credit for it belongs to a positivist and *Kulturkämpfer* named Karl Knortz (1841–1918). His *Geschichte der nordamerikanischen Literatur* (Berlin) contained ten pages of commentary on Thoreau, with the emphasis placed principally upon Thoreau in his role as abolitionist. Knortz's work evidently became the dominant model for Thoreau studies over the next two decades. Its form was that of the usual nineteenth-century German literary study. It consisted of a long biography followed by a summary of Thoreau's ideas on nature, abolition, and government. The whole was supported by lengthy quotations, and there was scarcely any critical analysis. When it is remembered, however, that the articles on Thoreau by his early reviewers and critics were dedicated to introducing him to a reading public which was previously unaware of his existence, the stereotyped form of presentation seems justifiable. It is unfortunate, however, that such presentations led to an emphasis upon only those parts of Thoreau's life and philosophy which it was thought would appeal most certainly to German readers. His views on slavery were constantly summarized, and it could very well be argued that had he not been involved in the John Brown episode, the underground railroad, and a famous refusal to pay taxes, his German reviewers of that time, including even Knortz, would have found little indeed to say about him.

The earliest German article on Thoreau to appear in a periodical was printed in 1892 ("H. D. Thoreau," *Beilage zur Allgemeinen Zeitung*, CXVI [18 May]). The author, Heinrich Noe, objected that no publisher had as yet brought out any of Thoreau's works. He suggested some explanations for this fact and he advanced reasons for translating and publishing Thoreau. In his appreciative introduction to Thoreau, he claimed that there were resemblances between Thoreau's ideas and those to which Jean Paul Richter had given fictional expression. And he maintained that Thoreau, although certainly not one who could subscribe to the doctrine of art for art's sake, had the stylistic ability of the French; in addition, he had the German capacity to discern the essence of nature. Whether Noe's article was the final inducement or not is impossible to say, but five years later the first translation of *Walden*, Emmerich's, was offered to the public.

Knortz's second excursion into Thoreau studies, *Ein amerikanischer Diogenes* (Hamburg, 1899) deviated but little from his established pattern. His thesis, that Thoreau was an "Anarchist des Idealismus" who attempted to combine the simplicity of nature with the complexities of human civilization, was nearly lost sight of in the mass of biography. Regrettably, the same criticism is almost as valid for the work of Carl Federn (1864–1943), journalist, anglophile, and internationalist who has sometimes been mistakenly credited with launching Thoreau's career in Germany. His "Henry David Thoreau" (*Monatsblätter des Wissenschaftlichen Club in Wien* [9 January 1899], reprinted as his chapter on Thoreau in the *Essays zur amerikanischen Litteratur* [Halle, 1899]) was, except for the comment that Thoreau was not so profound as Emerson nor so revolutionary as Whitman, little more than appreciative biography.

To the basic chords, variations were gradually added. One of those who offered amplifications on the theme was Josef Hofmiller. In his "Thoreau" (*Süddeutsche, Monatshefte* [February 1907] reprinted in *Versuche* [Munich, 1909]) he sought to popularize Thoreau and win him converts. In a well-written essay he covered the usual ground—Thoreau's attitude towards slavery, his ideas on government, his closeness to nature, and his philosophy as compared to Emerson's—but he also went farther. To him, this truly un-European writer who was presently in a middle position between obscurity and fame should not be thought of as simply a recluse. His ideas, which must have had their source in religious inspiration, lead us back to the essentials of life. Next to *Walden,* the closet dramas of the time seem idle and stale, and the stereotyped novels seem, in Hofmiller's terminology, "perfumed." In comparison with these, "This *Walden* is an unintentionally critical book."

At about this same time Franz Strunz of Vienna published two essays on Thoreau. The first ("Naturgefühl and Naturerkenntnis bei Henry David Thoreau," *Beitrage und Skizzen zur Geschichte der Naturwissenschaften* [Hamburg, 1909]) offered little that was not commonplace, but his second ("Das Fortschrittliche and Neue im Naturgefühl bei Henry David Thoreau," *Dokumente des Fortschritts* [March, 1910]) introduced the concept of Thoreau as a Kantian. What we call nature, wrote Strunz, is only a manifestation of the union of essence and appearance, or symbol. The laws or hypotheses we project into it form the proof of our souls. It is only subjectivity or spirit that creates. For Thoreau, the entire world was the embodiment of Idea; his philosophy of nature and of man was, in many respects, Kantian. Thus Thoreau was not simply a nature poet, but one whose subjective impressions were translated into natural contexts.

Some of the other variations on the theme of Thoreauvianism were not only less profound than Strunz's but also faintly derisive. One A. Prinzinger, in "Henry D. Thoreau, ein amerikanischer Naturschilderer" (Salzburg, 1895), wrote a long essay consisting almost entirely of quotations loosely strung together. The binder between the quotations was the idea that Americans are such a practical folk and so oblivious to the charms of nature that it is both an unexpected and pleasant surprise to discover an American, like Thoreau, who is truly a nature lover. Leon Kellner, in his *Geschichte der nordamerikanischen Literatur* (Berlin, 1913), saw no spiritual or intellectual justification whatever in the Walden experiment. To him, Thoreau was merely a practical and didactic writer with a poetic talent. Another leitmotiv, that Americans are for the most part so bent on conforming to each other in their common quest for riches that they seldom evince individuality as Thoreau had, was introduced by A. von Ende, at the time from Chicago, in his article for the *Beilage zur Allgemeinen Zeitung* (26 August 1896). These themes did not reappear during the first period of Thoreau's reception, but they were used in a diatribe printed about the beginning of the second World War.

The article which continued this line of criticism, one of the two which came out between the wars, was by Edgar Maass ("Thoreau," *Das innere Reich*, VI [1939]). In it, he presented as the villains American materialism, antipathy to natural beauty, and the "Nihilismus der amerikanischen Seele." America itself was the new democracy "which in these times has sought to conquer an entire continent, and which along the way—dear God—has become so quickly saturated, old, and narrow-minded." But Thoreau was the exception, and he was praised, the better to criticize his countrymen. The praise centered about Thoreau's sympathy for the Indians and his patriotism.

The other interim article was of a very different nature. Its title was "Thoreau als Befreier" (*Die Tat*, XII [1920]) and it was written by Paul Westphal. Prophesying worse yet to come if true values and ideals were not resurrected, Westphal wanted to revive post World War I Germany by renunciation of the false codes inherent in an over-mechanized and over-civilized existence. The actualities of inflation and impoverished urbanization, the threat of communism, the indifference to responsibility by the educated classes, and the fear of capitalistic exploitation, led him to suggest a bootstrap operation based upon a return-to-the-pond movement. It was to be supported by cooperative labor, interclass assistance, improved methods of farming, advanced technology, and moral regeneration founded upon altruism and curtailment of the human instinct to profit from another's misfortune. The blueprint for this was *Walden*. It was to have been to Westphal and other Germans seeking true freedom even more than "Civil Disobedience" had been for Gandhi and the Indians.

Between 1945 and 1951 Thoreau's writings were again published and scholarly investigations were resumed in 1948. Most critics apparently assumed that the need to introduce him was no longer so pressing, so studies took a somewhat different form. His abolitionism was never quite forgotten, of course, but comparative and even religious approaches tended to replace the biographical. The first essay after the war, "Der gerade Weg des H. D. Thoreau" by Fritz Krökel (*Der Speicher* [1948]), strongly emphasized both Thoreau's protest against the tyranny of the majority and his search for religious freedom. According to Krökel, this freedom consisted of unobstructed eclecticism in excerpting suitable doctrines from the Chinese, Indian, and Persian religions. That the elements of Thoreau's philosophy which exemplified his revolt against the coercion of the individual should have been stressed by a post-war German author is a reminder that political and social circumstances can seldom be divorced completely from the study of literature.

As the war years became more remote, studies of Thoreau decreased in number. Of the half-dozen articles printed during the post-war period, two by Johannes Urzidil were comparative studies which adduced resemblances between Stifter and Thoreau ("Adalbert Stifter und Henry Thoreau," *Welt und Wort* [1950] and "Weltreise in Concord," *Neue literarische Welt* [10 May 1953]— his "Henry David Thoreau oder Natur und Freiheit," *Castrum Peregrini*, XXX [1956] was along traditional, earlier lines, and in his "Stifter aus drei Distanzen," *Literatur und Kritik*, XXXI [February 1969] he repeated and enlarged upon his theme of the first two articles). The two were nearly contemporaries, their ideas were similar, they sometimes used the same images, and Thoreau was probably acquainted with Stifter's writings, particularly the *Hochwald*. Urzidil's essays were followed by a long and appreciative article by Stefan Andres ("Der Eremit von Walden Pond," *Perspektiven* [1955]) in which Thoreau's religion was once again examined. His theism was likened to that of St. Francis of Assisi, he was termed a nominalist, and his mysticism was convincingly equated to that of Meister Eckhart and the Zen Buddhists. Yet in conventional Christianity he found the sanctification for action and the courage to support rebellion and reform.

Ernst Schlick's "Henry David Thoreau: Ein Held der Vereinigten

Staaten" (*Zeitschrift für Geopolitik* [1959])is noteworthy only for its discussion of the political pragmatism of "Civil Disobedience," which was not published in translation until 1949. This was one of the few indications that German readers had first-hand knowledge of Thoreau's works other than *Walden* and a few selections from the *Journal*. On this more solid basis then, Germanic evaluations of Thoreau returned to one of their initial points of departure. It seems highly unlikely, however, that the cycle, once completed, will not repeat itself in different dimensions. At this point only the first chapter on the impact of Thoreau in Germany can be written. As Horst Oppel wisely observed in Kohlschmidt and Mohr's *Reallexikon der deutschen Literaturgeschichte* (Berlin, 1955), "his final effect has not yet been felt on either side of the Atlantic" (I, 58).

Henry D. Thoreau in Switzerland

Dominik Jost

DOMINIK JOST is from St. Gallen, Switzerland, where he has taught since 1953. He studied at the universities in Basel, Zürich, and Fribourg, where he received the doctoral degree in 1946. His interests have been recent German and foreign literatures, including American, and art. He has written on Stefan George, Ludwig Derleth, and the literature of the art nouveau movement; in addition, he has edited many other books, the latest of which is a six-volume edition of the works of Derleth. He has been a Visiting Professor at the University of Colorado and at McGill University, as well as Associate Professor at the University of Rochester.

HENRY D. THOREAU IN SWITZERLAND

During Thoreau's lifetime many Swiss looked upon the prospering United States of America with optimism and expectation. Nothing illustrates this better than the fact that within those forty-five years about 40,000 Swiss (out of a population of 2.5 million in 1850) emigrated to the new continent. Such emigration had its basis not only in faith but also in foreknowledge. In the 1820's numerous travel books and settlers' diaries had come out in the homeland.[1] Moreover, about thirty American newspapers and magazines were known in Switzerland at the time, and their occasional treatment of transcendentalism—seen as a combination of democratic freedom and romantic subjectivism—had a sympathetic audience among Swiss readers. In the 1850's American novels started flooding into Switzerland. Book reviewers in Swiss papers announced that America's new export goods were not only cotton and coffee, but also novels. Often they complained that the market was overfed, and with some justification. *Uncle Tom's Cabin*, the best example of this inundation, was published in ten versions during the second half of 1852 alone. In addition, speeches by William Ellery Channing, made in 1840, were translated and printed at Zürich/Winterthur as early as 1843, and Daniel Webster was mentioned in the press with unanimous admiration, sometimes even compared to George Washington.

There were, it must be admitted, a few contradictory elements to be found in the predominantly receptive attitude of the Swiss. In his sensational book, *Amerika ohne Schminke (America without*

---

1. Robert H. Billigmeier and Fred A. Picard have recently re-edited two especially instructive documents: English versions of Johannes Schweizer's and Johann Jakob Rütlinger's diaries. *The Old Land and the New. The Journals of Two Swiss Families in America in the 1820's* (Minneapolis, 1965).

Make-Up [Zürich, 1857]), Franz Josef Egenter presented press notices of criminal statistics which he had collected from American newspapers and magazines over a period of five years. His was not the only dissenting voice. There is, for instance, the following portrait of a swindler in Jeremias Gotthelf's (1797–1854) novel *Uli der Pächter* (*Uli as a Tenant Farmer*): "He had never been to where he boasted to have traveled; somewhere else he had borrowed money in Joggeli's name, and with that he had disappeared, probably like other rascals, to America" (chapter 23).

Despite such occurrences, American literature, as demonstrated by Emil Graf[2] and Robert Keiser,[3] met with growing interest in Switzerland during the nineteenth century. American bestsellers—novels and travel books in particular—were likely to be well received in Switzerland; at the same time, essayists, including Emerson, fared no better in Switzerland than they did in America. In spite of the generally favorable climate of interest in America, however, Thoreau was hardly known in Switzerland in his own time, a situation which seems not to be particularly surprising in view of the fact of his poor reception in his own country.

A look into the *Bibliographie der Gesellschaftsschriften, Zeitungen und Kalender in der Schweiz* (Bern, 1896), edited by Josef Leopold Brandstetter,[4] indicates that American writers must have encountered a climate which, by virtue of the overwhelming number of periodicals for literature and general culture, appeared favorable. If, however, we started sifting through this mass of documentary material, we should gain no knowledge of how the Swiss public reacted to Thoreau because he is mentioned only sporadically and

---

2. Emil Graf, *Die Aufnahme der englischen und amerikanischen Literatur in der deutschen Schweiz von 1800–1830* (Zürich, 1951).
3. Robert Keiser, *Die Aufnahme englischen und amerikanischen Schrifttums in der deutschen Schweiz von 1830 bis 1860* (Zürich, 1962). The manuscript is in the Zürich Zentralbibliothek, partly printed.
4. Josef Leopold Brandstetter's book of reference has been completed as the *Bibliographie der Schweizer Presse. Quellen zur Schweizer Geschichte*, by Fritz Blaser (Basel, 1956).

cursorily. In one representative newspaper, the *Neue Zürcher Zeitung*, the records of which extend back to 1871, Thoreau was mentioned only twice, both times in 1945[5] Both feuilletons were printed in connection with the printing of *Walden* in 1945.

In 1946 Walter Kern pointed out Thoreau's importance in the *Neue Schweizer Rundschau* (p. 238 ff.); obviously he assumed— he had to assume—that to his readers the American author was a complete stranger. Summing up, he said of Thoreau: "The essence of his works ... lies in his descriptions of nature. Only a true poet could write down the subtlest observations with such a perfect sureness in choosing his own words and metaphors, that sureness being a result of Thoreau's complete lack of preconceived notions. The genuine approach he found to everything—writing included— made for an ever-youthful personality."

For a Swiss whose native language is German, French, or Italian, and who is dependent upon the public libraries, it is not easy to get acquainted with Thoreau's books other than *Walden*. Nor is there to be found any text of Thoreau's at all which is dated earlier than 1881. A German version of *Walden* was first published in 1897 (Munich); further editions of the years 1902 (Munich), 1905 (Jena and Leipzig), 1914 (Berlin), and 1922 (Jena) can be found in Swiss public libraries. *Winter* came out in Munich in 1900 and by 1921 was in the third edition (Paderborn). Selections from the German texts were printed in 1947 (Vienna), 1949 (Vienna), and 1951 (Gütersloh). An Italian version of *Walden* was brought out in 1920 (Florence) and a French one in 1922 (Paris). *Opere scelte* from Thoreau's writings were published in 1958 (Venice) and "*Désobéir*" was produced in 1921 (Paris).

Up to now only three Thoreau editions have appeared in Switzerland, all of them in German: *Herbst (Autumn). From the Diary of Henry D. Thoreau*, edited by H. G. O. Blake. Translated from English by Bertha Engler, with the cooperation of Ernst Frey (Zür-

---

5. "Aus der Einleitung zu *Waldensee*" by Fritz Güttinger, page 1461; also "Leseprobe aus den Tagebüchern (*Walden*)," page 1954.

ich, 1943). *Walden.* With an Introduction and Annotations by Fritz Güttinger. Translated from English by Siegfried Lang (Zürich, 1945).

The foreword that Ernst Frey contributed to the Zürich edition of *Herbst* (5000 copies and out of print since 1951) is worth reading. In it, he relates that his enthusiastic veneration for Thoreau dates back to 1907, to his first encounter with *Walden.*

> In the summer of 1907, Professor Andreas Baumgartner in Zürich, my amiable patron for many years, sent Henry Thoreau's *Walden* to join me in the solitude in which I was then living. This was the message that came with it: "Here is a man for you. He must be to your taste." The book not only proved to offer the sheerest joy I had found up to then, but it also helped me much to justify my own existence. In gratitude, I vowed to the shades of Thoreau to do everything in my power to propagate his name and his works. . . . For his sake some of my friends then started learning English, a few of them even at an advanced age.

From the rest of the foreword it becomes apparent that Frey was profoundly impressed by Thoreau's ability to establish the freedom from want which would permit him to lead a life of the spirit, unbiased, independent, and with dignity; also the lack of a dualism which might have marred the consistency of his life and his thoughts. He praises Thoreau as a "self-saviour who does not need God or any gods."

To Siegfried Lang's version of *Walden*, Fritz Güttinger wrote the foreword. Here, genuine respect for Thoreau as a personality and as a writer is sometimes subtly mingled with our century's almost inevitable irony at the sight of a man who lives a life like Thoreau's. Most of all, Güttinger underlines Thoreau's original character, his bliss of ego which confines the universe to his own soul. Like Henry Seidel Canby, Güttinger understands *Walden* as the expression of a strongly utopian concept: "Together with all great Utopias, this vision of humanity reckons with a humanity that does not exist yet and perhaps never will."

Swiss literary critics have reacted neither to *Herbst* nor to *Wal-*

den. If the translators and editors had any hopes that the two Zürich editions would secure for Thoreau a standard place in the mind of the educated Swiss reader they have been disappointed. The cause may lie in the Swiss national character with its respect for civic mindedness and solidarity, its confidence in the idea of the political state, its leaning towards practicality and the sound middle course rather than towards experiments in individualistic living: in short, an a-romantic if not anti-romantic national soul. So Swiss journalism has quietly let the years 1917 and 1962 pass by without being prompted to commemorate Henry David Thoreau.

As a conclusion to this survey it should be mentioned that there is a very limited number of secondary works to be found in the libraries. There is a first study by A. Prinzinger (1895); then there are articles by Karl Knortz and Karl Federn (1899); there is an essay of 1909 by Josef Hofmiller (reprinted in 1911 in an anthology entitled *Versuche*) which appeared originally in the *Süddeutsche Monatshefte*; in addition there are articles by Adalbert Luntowski (1910), Emil Frey (1943), Fritz Güttinger (1945) and Walter Kern (1946—both of the foregoing mentioned above), and Eleonore Engelhardt (1963). By Guido Ferrando, the translator of *Walden*, we have a study in Italian (Venice, 1928), and there are French books by Léon Bazalgette (Paris, 1924) and Andrée Bruel (Paris, 1929). (The most recent Swiss work on the subject is *Henry David Thoreau: Über die Pflicht zum Ungehorsam gegen den Staat* [Zürich, 1967].)

The paucity of books by and about Thoreau in Switzerland testifies to the limitation of his influence. How difficult it is to prove the influence of Thoreau's writings on the intellectual life of Germany (which would imply Switzerland) can be seen from the way in which Lawrence Marsden Price dealt with this author each of the three times he edited his *English-German Literary Influences*.[6] In the 1919 edition Thoreau is briefly mentioned in connection with

---

6. (Berkeley, 1919). Second edition, *The Reception of English Literature in Germany* (1932). Third edition, *English Literature in Germany* (1953). See also his *The Reception of United States Literature in Germany* (Chapel Hill, 1966).

Emerson, and there is the remark about Karl Federn's Thoreau essay: "With Emerson and Whitman, Federn groups Thoreau among America's great originals. His studies of nature and his philosophy of life seem to have attracted relatively little attention in Germany despite Federn's essay and a translation of *Walden*, which had appeared two years before" (p. 575); obviously, Price then did not know Josef Hofmiller's study on Thoreau. In the vastly revised edition of 1932, Thoreau is eliminated (though other Americans, Emerson for instance, are mentioned again); and as might be expected, he is kept out of the 1953 edition too.

Anyone who has ever examined the products of the average Swiss general education must have looked in vain for traces of Thoreau. Even people specialized in philosophical or literary studies (except if they happen to be or have been Anglicists or Americanists) fail to produce any remotely satisfactory associations with his name. Each of the "happy few" who can appreciate him has discovered him on his own; it is as individuals that they have met with this individualist. Thoreau's lack of doctrinarianism kept him from putting his own idea of the right way of life too rigorously into practice, for after all, he never thought of setting up a nature school, of starting a movement, or of founding a sect.

In Switzerland the issue of Thoreau's influence is subject to further confusion. We must be suspicious of ascribing to him an influence which is more likely to have been exerted by one who often spoke in the same vein—Jean-Jacques Rousseau from Geneva. The reformative ideas of Rousseau are generally known (although not so generally practiced) by every high school student. So we should seldom be right if we expected to find Thoreau's ideas at the bottom of the numerous experiments in a new style of natural, anti-progressionist living such as has been practiced, most notably, in the Canton of Tessin, e.g., on Monte Verità near Ascona. To discover Thoreau's influence at work wherever modern civilization has been criticized in his spirit would be mistaken. There are, after all, striking, genuinely Swiss parallels to his nature gospel, his respect for the rights and the dignity of the individual, his reformist ideas.

Where he has been accepted in Switzerland at all, he could hardly do more than confirm a conception of life that had at least partially existed before. Josef Hofmiller's statement about Thoreau, "in fact there is something thoroughly un-European about him" must be largely discounted; otherwise the personality and work of Rousseau would have to be called un-European too. Rousseau's views of a reformation of life, his political theses, his summons to return to nature, his liberal pedagogy, and his style of living, are all deeply imbedded in the Swiss consciousness; so a Swiss reader of Thoreau will always hear, or believe he hears, Rousseau's familiar voice, and only at a second listening may he become aware of the difference.

All of this does not, of course, exclude Thoreau's being occasionally mentioned *expressis verbis* and cited by those who know and appreciate him. As might be expected, most of them are themselves cultural philosophers. The majority are concerned about man's denaturalization, his growing inhuman rhythm of life, the impoverishment of his soul, and his way of sacrificing fulfillment in return for altogether questionable "progress." One of these critics is Hans Zbinden (born 1894 and professor at Bern University). On several occasions, in lectures and writings about the problematic conception of values in the technical era, he has cited Thoreau as king's evidence for his claims. He writes, for instance, "It is a symptomatic and gratifying sign that the impulse towards rethinking does not come only from the world of humanistic culture. More than a hundred years ago, Thoreau, the author of the enchanting book, *Walden*, said: 'Our inventions are but improved means to an un-improved end.' Today, Thoreau's opinion has been confirmed by the London economist, Professor Schumacher, member of the British Coal Board; in a lecture given in Vienna he said: 'The characteristics of the modern situation are an extraordinary wealth of means, and an extraordinary lack of incentives.' "[7] Speaking of Thoreau's position in the minds of the Swiss public, Hans Zbinden admits that "In the whole course of my activity as a professor at Bern University, as a

---

7. Hans Zbinden, *Kulturaufgaben der Wirtschaft in heutiger Zeit* (Düsseldorf, 1965).

lecturer in highly varied cultural circles, as a writer, and as a reader, I have never come across the name of Thoreau at all. Neither his name nor anything from his works is known. The name is hecuba to the young generation in general, and to students in particular. Lecturing, I have very often quoted Thoreau and talked about *Walden* in connection with man's cultural situation in a technical world. I then had to spell out Thoreau's name so that my audience knew of whom I was speaking. . . . In Swiss publications I have never met with any mention of Thoreau except for the bare name without further commentary."[8]

In our time there is in Switzerland a growing number of voices warning us that mere cultural activity, devoid of the meaning of what we understand culture to be, cheats man out of the only thing he has—human life. It is easy to see the physiognomy of our century is more and more growing into the faceless mask of the uniformed masses. But at the same time there exists, and perhaps grows, a group which knows the values now at stake. But the extent to which Thoreau's thoughts have been at work here, like an enlivening underground spring, cannot be traced easily; the information from our documentary material supports suppositions only, not conclusions.

Yet, since Thoreau's message obviously brings answers to urgent questions of our own time, it is important that his work be remembered now. Mankind is no longer so rich that it can thoughtlessly afford to ignore Thoreau's intense voice during these decades of crisis.

8. From a letter of 21 February 1966 to Dominik Jost.

Thoreau in Italy

Agostino Lombardo

AGOSTINO LOMBARDO is Professor of English and American literature at the Facoltá di Lettere of the University of Rome. He is Director of *Studi Americani*, and his publications include works on Hawthorne and James. His American essays are collected in *Realismo e Simbolismo* and *La Licerca del Vero*. His most recent book is on *Macbeth*.

THOREAU IN ITALY

On the publication of the Italian translation of Thoreau's Selected Works in 1958[1] (the first and only translation of *Walden* dated back to 1920)[2] Emilio Cecchi, both an exquisite essayist and a real connoisseur of American and English literature, accurately observed that Thoreau had been among the American authors most neglected in Italy. "During our youth," he wrote, "few read him. But he was cited more than read—and cited erroneously as a mere by-product of Emerson who, only through his connection with Carlyle, had a certain number of followers among us. Finally, then, it was the living legend of Thoreau much more than his writing which caught our interest and received some attention."[3] And, actually, whoever follows the "career" of American literature in Italy will note that with the exception of Melville and Emily Dickinson, discovered rather late in their own country, the major American writers were translated or discussed or at least relatively well-known at sometimes astonishingly early dates: Franklin, already translated in 1774 (in what is probably the first American book translated in Italian);[4] Washington Irving, 1824; Fenimore Cooper, 1827—and from then on his "career" in Italy is only matched by Harriet Beecher Stowe's[5] or, in poetry, Longfellow's; writings on Poe begin in

1. H. D. Thoreau, *Opere Scelte*, ed. by P. Sanavio (Venice 1958). See later in this essay.
2. H D. Thoreau, *Walden*, transl. by G. Ferrando (Florence 1920).
3. E Cecchi, *Scrittori Inglesi e Americani*, 2 vols. (Milan 1954), I. pp. 103–7.
4. The title of the book, a selection of Franklin's letters and pamphlets, is: *Scelta di lettere e di opuscoli del signor Beniamino Franklin tradotti dall'inglese* (Milan 1774).
5. On the Italian fortune of Cooper and Harriet Beecher Stowe see the articles by James Woodress: "The fortunes of Cooper in Italy," *Studi Americani*, 11 (Rome 1965), pp 53–76, and *Uncle Tom's Cabin* in Italy," in *Essays on American Literature in Honor of Jay B. Hubbell*, ed. by Clarence Gohdes (Durham, 1967), pp. 126–40.

1856 while the first of a long and uninterrupted series of translations already appears in 1848; for the first time Whitman is discussed in print in 1879 and *Leaves of Grass* is translated in 1887; Hawthorne's slow but steady "career" begins between 1860 and 1870 while Mark Twain's, quicker and often overwhelming, is initiated in 1891; James is translated late, but by 1880 something is already known of him; translations of Howells came extremely late, only a few years ago, but we find some allusion to his fiction as early as 1884[6]; Emerson, who is first cited in 1847 and first translated in 1865, ranks among those writers most frequently translated and discussed; he penetrates to the very heart of Italian culture.[7]

We would think, then, that Thoreau would soon follow along in Emerson's tracks and enjoy an early reputation in Italy. Yet this is not the case. It is only in 1884 that we find any information on him, clearly second-hand, and, moreover, so inaccurate that it does more damage than good to any attempt at an understanding of the writer. In his history of American literature, 1884,[8] Gustavo Strafforello (who also has the distinction of being Hawthorne's first translator and is among the first to translate Emerson) places Thoreau, first of all, among the "scientists and philosophers," defining him as a "naturalist in the transcendental school of Emerson" who

---

6. On Poe see Ada Giaccari, "La fortuna di Poe in Italia," *Studi Americani*, 5 (Rome 1959), pp. 91–118; on Whitman, M. Meliado', "La fortuna di Walt Whitman in Italia," *Studi Americani*, 7 (1961), pp. 43–76; on Hawthorne, C. Zauli-Naldi, "La fortuna di Hawthorne in Italia," *Studi Americani*, 6 (1960), pp. 183–201; on Mark Twain, C. Consiglio, "La fortuna di Mark Twain in Italia," *Studi Americani*, 4 (1958), pp. 198–208.

More general information can be found in M. Bignami, "La letteratura americana in Italia," *Studi Americani*, 10 (1964), pp. 443–95. For the period 1945–1954 see *Repertorio bibliografico della letteratura americana in Italia*, ed. by B. M. Tedeschini Lalli, 2 vols., (Rome, 1966).

A general introduction (and a selected bibliography) in A. Lombardo, "La letteratura americana in Italia," in *La Ricerca del Vero*, Saggi sulla Tradizione Letteraria Americana (Rome, 1961), pp. 13–61.

7. See R. Anzilotti, "Emerson in Italia," *Rivista di Letterature Moderne e Comparate* (March 1958), pp. 3–14, and M. T. De Majo, "La fortuna di Ralph Waldo Emerson in Italia," *Studi Americani*, 13 (1966), pp. 45–87.

8. G. Strafforello, *Storia della letteratura americana* (Milan, 1884).

in his writings (among which *Walden* is not mentioned) "glorified American nature." Strafforello goes on, placing particular emphasis on the "legend" of which Cecchi spoke ("Scientific and rustic at the same time, he lived and wrote for many years in a little wooden cabin which he himself built in the middle of the woods!") and his "familiarity with the animals of the forest and with silent nature." Given the still embryonic state of knowledge of American literature in Italy, the following characterization of transcendentalism by Strafforello is not without interest; Thoreau, however, remains a mere name, one of the shadows (though they were select shadows) which followed Emerson:

> Emerson was the founder of a school. And about this thinker, this Plato brought back from the dead, there drew a circle of men and women—Hawthorne, Alcott, Thoreau, Channing, Margaret Fuller-Ossoli, etc.—from which was born in 1830 and in the following years that intellectual movement known as Transcendentalism which put to rest orthodox puritanism, aged and narrow-minded, and restored the liberty of its own religious sentiment to the soul of the American people. These same transcendentalists stirred the sleeping conscience of the nation against Negro slavery and were the inspiration behind the Abolition Movement which brought about the War of Secession and, as a result, victory for the cause of humanity.

Carlo Salsa's history of American literature[9] which, not specifically dated, must have appeared in the opening decade of the twentieth century, literally copied Strafforello's work but left out certain sections—Thoreau was thus eliminated, reappearing as a pure and simple follower of Emerson, at times only as a bibliographical item, in that large quantity of writings on Emerson done between the end of the nineteenth and beginning of the twentieth centuries.[10]

Surprisingly, on the other hand, Thoreau is the object of a study which if not profound is certainly a labor of love: this is *L'America*

---

9. C. Salsa, *La letteratura nord-americana* (Milan n.d.).
10. See above, note 7. A description of Walden pond and of Thoreau's tomb can be found in *America Vittoriosa* (Milan 1899), by Ugo Ojetti, a famous journalist who had written a series of articles on the United States.

nella Letteratura by Giacinto Chimenti,[11] an almost completely unknown man of letters from the provinces. The booklet was published in Bari and as the subtitle explains is actually an essay devoted to Thoreau. Again we have no specific publication date; the booklet's tone, though (which in its fiery anti-positivistic polemics is reminiscent of Benedetto Croce's early writings), the references to Enrico Nencioni (a distinguished litterateur who at the end of the nineteenth century wrote on American and English literature with great subtlety and who, strangely enough, never concerned himself with Thoreau), the references to Strafforello, and a number of other hints place this first example of criticism on Thoreau somewhere around 1910. In truth, however, the booklet is more of an *apologia* than it is a critical essay; it is a passionate defense of Thoreau from any possible accusation of "egotism," "anarchism," or "cynicism"; it is an exaltation of the man ("we now lack men of Thoreau's stature") and of the writer ("he was one of the greatest, most gifted Americans, a powerful and absolute genius") whose major work, *Walden*, "should be read at least once a year." And still, at the same time, Chimenti is able to combine this enthusiasm with a real understanding of Thoreau's work: the intuition of his identity an an American, his *"americanità"*; his feeling for the "relationships with things"; his spirit of observation ("He observed everything as through a microscope, reproducing each object which he saw or felt with the accuracy of a photograph"). It is regrettable that the author's limited reputation and the almost private character of his booklet never forced it from the confines of the provinces.

We must wait until 1919, then, to find another study of Thoreau: an article by Anna Benedetti which appears in the authoritative *Nuova Antologia*[12] and which unfortunately limits itself to reporting American opinions and sketching of major biographical facts. It is only in 1920 that the first translation of *Walden*, rendered by

---

11. G. Chimenti, *L'America nella Letteratura (Thoreau)* (Bari, n.d.). In 1884 Felice Chimenti had published in Bari *Note di letteratura americana*.
12. A. Benedetti, "Henry David Thoreau, il solitario di Walden," *Nuova Antologia*, 16 March 1919.

Guido Ferrando,[13] finally appears. The book is accompanied by neither an introduction nor any information on the author; the quality of the translation, though, is notably high (Ferrando was also a careful and competent scholar to which his writings on Emerson testify) and thus Italian readers can approach Thoreau through a version which not only does not betray his character but which, on the contrary, is faithful to the text and to the spirit of the author.

It is impossible to say what circulation *Walden* had among the public; we can certainly say, however, that Ferrando's fine work left no traceable mark on Italian culture. There are only a few exceptions, incidental references to be found in works on Emerson, Whitman, etc. In 1936 the silence is interrupted by a brief and vague profile sketched by Giacomo Prampolini in his *Storia Universale della Letteratura*[14] and a little later, in 1939 by a fleeting voice in the *Enciclopedia Italiana*.[15] Still they did practically nothing to boost the circulation or contribute to a greater understanding of Thoreau. In these two decades we see the development of the Italian knowledge of American literature into something much vaster and deeper, due especially to the critical and scholarly works of Carlo Linati, Emilio Cecchi and Mario Praz;[16] meanwhile, in the years around 1930, America exercised more than a literary attraction: for anti-Fascist writers like Elio Vittorini and Cesare Pavese it held a political and ideological attraction which would result in the American literary experience becoming a live and active part of the Italian experience. Yet through this fervor of studies and discoveries Thoreau remains nearly unknown. Melville and Hawthorne, Poe and Whitman and Emerson—they are all studied, all translated; Emily Dickinson is discovered; not only are the modern classics like Hemingway and Faulkner translated, but also minor authors who were perhaps not even worthy of the attention. In order to read something that is

13. See note 2.
14. (Turin 1936).
15. (Rome 1939).
16. See A. Lombardo, *op. cit.*, and also Donald Heiney, *America in Modern Italian Literature* (New Brunswick 1964).

more than incidental on Thoreau we must go all the way to 1941, to the historical notes on American literature written by Elio Vittorini which preface the anthology *Americana*, an anthology so markedly anti-Fascist that it was immediately suppressed.[17] Vittorini also speaks of Thoreau together with Emerson, but this time he is clearly something more than a simple marginal figure, indeed he is a three-dimensional character, an authentic protagonist:

> ... with Emerson, with Thoreau, the great contradiction which goes by the name of America began to reveal itself. ... Culture in these men was as deep and strong as in the most civilized men in Europe, Carlyle and Goethe. Ralph Waldo Emerson was not satisfied with assimilating contemporary thought; he took over at first hand Plato, Plotinus and Montaigne, together with all that had remained contemporary in the writers of the past. In the same way Henry Thoreau meditated on Greek texts, discussing them with himself in the diary which was both his life and his work, and, by continually readjusting his sense of values, chose among the many juices which form the sap of human knowledge. But this assimilation in them led, in the end, to genuine expression; it became what it had been trying for a long time to become—expression. Full, at last, and absolute: expression through assimilation. With some of Emerson's *Essays*, and some poems ..., with Thoreau's *Walden* (a small part of the *Journals*), it was in America that human consciousness took a new step forward. Emerson and Thoreau said a little more than Europeans had said up to their time. More than Goethe: about the individual, about the personality, about the moral life and about God. More than Carlyle: on history. Emerson's theory of art as the expression of experience and his revealing on a higher level of truth is, fundamentally, still alive today. His other theory touching "self-reliance," the proclamation of non-conformity, and Tho-

---

17. A second edition was published in 1942 (Milan) with an introduction by E. Cecchi. Vittorini published his introductory notes, with additions, in *Diario in Pubblico* (Milan, 1957). On Vittorini and American literature see A. Lombardo, "L'America di Vittorini," in *La Ricerca del Vero*, pp. 63–81, and V. Amoruso, "Cecchi, Vittorini, Pavese e la letteratura americana," *Studi Americani*, 6 (1960), pp. 9–71.

reau's theory of civil disobedience were only worthily taken up many years later.

Here we can see the influence of Lawrence's *Studies in Classic American Literature* which was well-known in Italy. (Lawrence, it should be noted, had ignored Thoreau and this can help explain why it took the New Englander so long to "arrive" in Italy.) At the same time, though, the Sicilian writer displays a stylistic and moral quality which is quite his own. In this same provocative section Vittorini continues:

> Yet they spoke coldly, with ice on their lips. The loud new voice raised in them a metaphysical roar, without revealing the wild animal. And they enriched human consciousness in intellect alone, not in the blood: they enriched it with abstract fury.
>
> A further step forward was needed: it was necessary to reach Poe, Hawthorne and Melville to arrive at concrete words. These writers worked in the blood, with blood, and set free the new force in all its strength. They were not held back by the timidities that checked earlier writers, including Emerson and Thoreau. What was there in man? Was there rottenness, sickness and damnation? "L'Amérique est pourrie," Cooper's Frenchmen had said, "avant d'être mûre." It had "putrified" because it lived on prejudices, conventions and inhibitions. But the body contained a bitter voice, savage, uncivilized, not in the least "mature," the voice of youthful ferocity. Here lay the great contradiction and Thoreau and Emerson, as I have said, had begun to draw it from its ancestral darkness. Slaves, however, themselves of prejudices, conventions and inhibitions, even while proclaiming the necessity of freeing man, they could only teach passive defence, and separation, abstraction, individual solitude. Their teaching was once again in favour of a "purity" which was a limitation to life, like that of the Puritans. And the contradiction, though revealed, was neither explained nor admitted. It was not recognized. They recognized, for example, that America, the new world, in order to be a new world (and the reaffirmation of man in the world) must absorb the "whole" of the old world. They recognized this, yet excluded suffering and evil from this "whole." Poe,

Hawthorne, and Melville instead accepted this suffering and evil first of all.... And they explained the contradiction. They showed that it was vital: a great contradiction.[18]

This is an exciting concept of American literature which could always be discussed and still contain a substantial element of truth. Still, here the more urgent observation is that Vittorini had placed Thoreau in the organic context of American literary culture (and not only American) of the nineteenth century and that his work, therefore, is not at all constricted by the limits of "naturalism" but rather considered in its true light—as a work which moves from the observation and representation of nature towards the poetic expression of much vaster and more universal search.

Italian culture was hastened still further in this direction by F. O. Matthiessen's *American Renaissance* (1941), that memorable critical and historical work which, although translated in 1954, had already strongly influenced the more alert Italian critics writing immediately after the war (and all the more so since one could easily detect the imprint of Francesco De Sanctis's *Storia della Letteratura Italiana* which Matthiessen had professedly taken as his own model). Cesare Pavese, in a 1946 essay significantly entitled "American Ripeness," wrote:

> We were accustomed to consider the United States a country which had introduced a passionate voice into world culture, a voice which was persuasive and unique only in the decade following the Great War. And the voices of Dewey and Mencken, Lee Masters and Sandburg, Anderson, O'Neill, Van Wyck Brooks, Waldo Frank, Gertrude Stein, Dreiser, Carlos Williams, Hemingway and Faulkner all seemed a sudden explossion, inexplicable and unexpected, of a social and academic crust which, except for occasional protests and breakaways (we knew something of Poe and Whitman), had existed intact since the beginnings of the colonies. Finally, though, it was not

---

18. The Vittorini passages have been translated by B. Arnett Melchiori, translator of an issue of the *Sewanee Review* (Summer 1960) entirely dedicated to "Italian Criticism of American Literature" and edited by A. Lombardo.

American culture which was renewing itself in those years; it was we who were touching it seriously with our own hands for the first time. Now a day does not pass in which voices from across the Atlantic do not zealously arrive, voices which recall, evoke and explain all of a rich, secular tradition in which at least already one great revolt, one great "renaissance," had taken place.[19]

Pavese only quickly comments on the parts of Matthiessen's book concerning Thoreau, lingering longer on those sections dealing with Melville and Whitman. It should be noted, though, that he considers Thoreau, along with Melville and Whitman as the most "vigorous" of the five writers, underlining "the character or organic immediacy" in Thoreau's prose and the "impeccability" of his style. The major contribution of this essay, it must also be said, is the identification which Pavese accomplishes, using Matthiessen as a guide, of the central motives of the American Renaissance and especially of the symbolic dimension of American literature:

> With the universe conceived as an Emersonian or Whitmanesque mine of emblems and absolute facts which the new Adam need only name or evoke in order to have it come to life, it is clear how more varied and much richer the living senses will become; the panorama, the spiritual forest which forces itself into the light will be revealed to such greater depths, to such deeper understanding. That multiplicity of undesirable things perceived in this new fineness will offer an always richer hatchery of symbols. As for the rest, the American tendency to discern a spiritual significance in every fact is also implicit in Emerson's transcendentalism. It dates back to the nation's religious origins, to its seventeenth century feeling of the hand of Providence, divine indignation, in the most mundane and private affairs....

It is precisely this identification which leads to Pavese's insights into the American literary experience of both the nineteenth and twentieth centuries and also leads to serious Italian criticism, going

19. Now collected in *La letteratura americana e altri saggi* (Turin, 1953), pp. 177–87. The preface by Italo Calvino is an excellent essay on Pavese and American literature. See also Amoruso, *op. cit.*

beyond the discovery stage, of major nineteenth century authors and of Thoreau. This is proved, more than by the pages devoted to Thoreau in several literary histories,[20] by a book on Thoreau due to Biancamaria Tedeschini Lalli which appeared in 1954.[21] Professor Tedeschini Lalli's work is richly polemical, interesting and perceptive; her thesis, in part, is concerned with shattering Thoreau's "myth," the kind of myth Emerson had delineated in his famous discourse in which he celebrated his deceased "disciple" as a "romantic hero." It is just this portrait of a "romantic hero" which she has set out to destroy, and she is frequently correct; often, however, the destruction of the myth also involves destroying something beyond the myth; in order to eliminate the "hero," the "romantic" must also be eliminated and Thoreau is stripped of attributes which belong to the culture from which he has emerged and which, while characterizing him historically, have a further validity which cannot be denied by the fact that they belong to the past. In effect, the book rightfully seeks to refute the "legend" built around Thoreau; yet there is an excessive tendency to discredit those actions out of which the legend was born: Thoreau's political and social ideas appear to the critic as pure and simple "fantasies" which can have "a justification and an aesthetical value" but from which "no important upheaval of moral or social character can be expected." This is only true if one seeks an "upheaval" as a result of a political idea, but not if one seeks a contribution to the liberty and dignity of the individual. In this sense Thoreau's ideas, even if considered as "attitudes" and "gestures" are much more than fantasies and, if they have not created an "upheaval," they have certainly left their mark on the American and democratic conscience. (This becomes even

---

20. G. Grillo, *Letterature straniere* (Turin, 1945). L. Somma, *Storia della letteratura americana* (Rome 1946). L. Berti, *Storia della letteratura americana*, 2 vols. (Milan, 1950). S Policardi, *Breve storia della letteratura anglo-americana* (Milan-Varese 1951). In 1951 an article on Thoreau by G. Visentin appeared in *La Fiera Letteraria*, 36 ("Rivalutazione di H. D. Thoreau").
21. B. M. Tedeschini Lalli, *Henry David Thoreau* (Rome 1954).

clearer when we think of the influence of Thoreau's ideas on Gandhi and the extent to which they can be felt in many current protest movements today.)

The book is thus limited by its own polemics which could be called anti-Emersonian. Its virtues are above all to be found in the subtlety with which Thoreau's work is examined in a literary context. Here the contribution is substantial and Professor Tedeschini Lalli, following a course first set by Matthiessen (whose book in an Italian version appeared in the same year),[22] moves with full independence and originality. One might point to some of her keen observations: the profound rapport which she, more than Matthiessen, sees between Thoreau and the Metaphysical writers, speaking, as she does, of a "true congeniality" between the American writer and the seventeenth century poets; her comments on Thoreau's attitude toward popular language which she feels, again differing with Matthiessen, has little effect on "his style of classical intonation" and does not disturb its "controlled equilibrium." Other critical insights are expressed in Italy for the first time, but are also important in an absolute sense, in as far as they bring attention to bear on the stylistic element and on Thoreau's linguistic consciousness, which is well exemplified by "the careful use of his own vocabulary," the "absolute mastery of his own sentences," the "intelligent and secure knowledge of the limits and expressive possibilities of means as simple as punctuation." Too, there are fine sections devoted to Thoreau's poetic production and, even more satisfying, examinations of his prose, especially in the one dealing with *Walden.*

After this book, both a first conclusion of the sparse observations and researches of the previous years and a point of reference for future studies, the history of Thoreau's Italian "career" becomes livelier; there is more activity, more results. In 1955 appears an important article by Claudio Gorlier[23] which we will look at later.

22. F. O. Matthiessen, *Rinascimento Americano,* transl. by F. Lucentini (Turin 1954).
23. C. Gorlier, "Thoreau e gli uomini," *Aut-Aut,* 25 (1955). See note 31.

Meanwhile, in *Budding America*, essays for a university course in 1956, Glauco Cambon renders an interpretation of Thoreau, the refinement of which cannot be ignored.[24] Here is the annotation on the final passage of "the Pond in Winter" in *Walden*:

> The movement of this passage . . . shows Thoreau at his best. It is a movement from particular things—the ice and water of Walden Pond, imaginatively observed in its hues, physical properties and behavior—to the universal reality of the mind; from an unknown particular place—Walden—to an ever wider horizon encompassing far-off shores and the whole inhabited world; from the frozen presence of ice to the fluid life of omnipresent water—Emerson's perennial flux; and from a particular moment in time as lived by a single consciousness in a given place, to all of human history, into the timeless. The metamorphosis of ice and water is a symbol of human imagination, enlivening all, bringing all back from the death of abstraction to life of perception; but this symbol is not created by a superimposition of abstract patterns to concrete reality. It naturally springs from the inner core of that reality as realized by a contemplative mind in quest of essences.

The histories of American literature linger longer on Thoreau than they had in the past: Salvatore Rosati's (1956)[25] recognizes in Thoreau "a balance between the senses and the intellect, thus creating a greater writer"; Carlo Izzo's (1957) particularly stresses the political aspect of Thoreau's work and, in addition, points to what he considers a fundamental contradiction:

> It is both annoying and sad that the vigorous supporter of Emancipation, the man who had raised his voice in praise and defense of John Brown, could then align himself with the most narrow-minded bourgeoisie, proving himself incapable of understanding that economic poverty and moral misery go hand-in-hand, and that one cannot pretend to find a nobility

---

24. Published in Milan. A much less original University lecture is "An Approach to Thoreau," by S. Fiorino (Catania 1957).
25. S. Rosati, *Storia della letteratura americana* (Turin 1956). A second edition in 1967.

of sentiments and a taste for beautiful things in people who, born in a hovel, have always been living by their wits. . . .[26]

But the most substantial product of the new interest in Thoreau stirred by Matthiessen's book and Tedeschini Lalli's monograph is the volume of Selected Works (*Opere Scelte*) which, edited by Piero Sanavio, makes its appearance in 1958.[27] For the first time since 1920 *Walden* is retranslated and it is accompanied by first translations of *A Natural History of Massachusetts, A Week, Cape Cod, Civil Disobedience, An Apology for John Brown*; the portrait of Thoreau now offered to the Italian public is, if not complete, certainly livelier and more profound, a result of Sanavio's long and complex introduction. This is divided into three sections: the first explains, clearly and precisely, the thought or, better stated, the poetics of transcendentalism; the second deals with Thoreau himself, his life, and his "career." Here Sanavio argues along with Tedeschini Lalli's book, strongly opposing the vision of Thoreau as an "aesthete," while in describing the writer's development he gives prominent stress (and this is a new critical insight in Italy) to that rapport with the Chinese philosophers and particularly Confucius which is seen as the pivot about which Thoreau's ideas revolve:

> If the Kung (of Confucius) maintained that "from this root, from this harmony the sky and the earth are established in their precise modality and the multitude of creatures exist nurtured in their glory," Thoreau for his part, exclaimed: "I see, smell, taste, hear, feel, that everlasting Something to which we are allied, at once our maker, our abode, our destiny, our very Selves; the one historic Truth, the most remarkable fact which can become the distinct and uninvited thought, the actual glory

---

26. C. Izzo, *Storia della letteratura nord-americana* (Milan 1957). A second edition in 1967 (Izzo also edited an anthology of American literature: *Le più belle pagine della letteratura nord-americana* [Milan, 1959]). A good history is also that by R. Anzilotti, *Storia della letteratura americana* (Milan 1957), while that by M. Hazon, *Storia della letteratura americana*, (Milan 1957) provides only outlines and that by G. Savelli, *Letteratura americana* (Rome 1956), is both erratic and sketchy.
27. See note 1.

of the universe; the only fact which a human being cannot avoid recognizing, or in some way forget or dispense with." It is precisely here that Thoreau parts company with Emerson; and this, then, is the level on which his work must be accepted and understood.

In the third and most challenging section Thoreau is viewed as an artist and, even more, as a "storyteller." Perhaps Sanavio goes too far in his examination of Thoreau's work as fiction; the comparisons of *A Week* to *Ulysses* and of *Walden*, at least in certain places, to *Finnegans Wake*, are somewhat strained. There is certainly nothing strained, however, about the concept which sees Thoreau not merely as an essayist, or a diarist (even considering the journals his life's *magnum opus*), or a writer describing natural scenes, but rather as a creative artist, one who does not limit himself to reproducing reality, but actually represents that reality poetically and therefore transforms it and, in this sense, truly "narrates" it.

Such a point of view is affirmed and developed by the present writer in a 1959 commentary-essay on the Selected Works[28] which insists on the presence in Thoreau of the "same impulse of artistic creation and conscious pursuit that gives rise to the art of Hawthorne or Melville" while affirming that Thoreau's "landscape" is one representing "life . . . not only nature" and that his work is a "unity of feeling, an existential totality." But the Selected Works leads to the appearance of a number of other articles, among which the most interesting are those by Emilio Cecchi and Marisa Bulgheroni. We had quoted from Cecchi's essay earlier;[29] now it should be added that he welcomes the possibility offered to Italian culture of better familiarizing itself with "a personality which was not, as generally regarded, monotonous and void of vital interests, but rather one which precociously anticipated ideological and aesthetic attitudes, several of which have only matured with writers of our

---

28. "L'arte narrativa di Thoreau," in *La Ricerca del Vero*, pp. 125–43 (appeared as an article in *Belfagor* [November 1959]). See also "La natura e l'uomo," in *Il Mondo* (March 1962).
29. See note 3.

own time." It is, in any case, the qualities of the writer and not the thinker which primarily attract Cecchi's attention ("Thoreau's truest strength is one of a pure writer"); he seems, then, to recognize in Thoreau's art that *gusto* for the "fragment" which has characterized twentieth century Italian prose:

> . . . much more than a builder, Thoreau is a courier, an explorer who at times is distracted and wanders in other directions. His art and his thought assume a major prominence and brilliance in the scraps and fragments, in the hustle and bustle of his fantastic adventure which lacks any architectural firmness or stateliness.

Marisa Bulgheroni,[30] for her part, emphasizes Thoreau's "vigorous love of reality," his "complete need of reality" and that aesthetic and moral consistency which prevents him from choosing either a "precise profession" or a "definite form of expression"; Thoreau's work, she further maintains, is also a lesson for our age and in his nature there is "a nature that each of us still feels very close to, an ideal form of existence which could be aimed at if only we could rouse ourselves from that 'calm desperation' in which Thoreau saw his own neighbors immersed."

Claudio Gorlier's *L'Universo Domestico*,[31] published in 1962, is the most important and challenging Italian contribution to the understanding of the "culture and society of New England in the nineteenth century." It distinguishes, clearly and perceptively, those rich and thick threads which are woven into the cultural and social fabric as central to Thoreau's thought and art. The book is full of penetrating pages dealing with Thoreau where Gorlier investigates and develops critical insights already expressed, as we have mentioned,

30. "Thoreau, il vagabondo," in *Il Demone del Luogo* (Milan-Varese, 1968), pp. 31–35 (appeared as an article in *Comunità* [October 1958]).
31. C. Gorlier, *L'Universo Domestico: Studi sulla cultura e la società della Nuova Inghilterra nel secolo XIX*, (Rome 1962). The chapter on Emerson and Thoreau included the essay already mentioned (see note 23).
    An article on Thoreau by G. Gullace had appeared in *Rivista di Letterature Moderne e Comparate* (September 1961) entitled *"Walden* e l'umorismo di Thoreau."

in 1955, the most interesting of which stress the importance of human values to Thoreau ("In the description of nature and in natural terms it is man who is most fully realized" . . . "Also Thoreau, like Emerson, proposes the construction of his own cosmology, but one which is more direct, more closely tied to man"). The most stimulating insights are those which underline Thoreau's identity as an American, his "*americanità*":

> Thoreau ostentatiously rejects non-American contributions, or, in the case of Oriental thought he introduces them into a genuinely American fabric, into the virgin landscape which he has rediscovered. It is he, before and more resolutely than Whitman in *American Vistas*, with whom the proudest American message arrives from the new continent.

And elsewhere:

> The new Adam, innocent and brave, is the symbolic character which Thoreau consigns to American culture. A single unity of theme, a landscape, a portrait of man, together with a style which, nourished at the wellspring of puritanical rhetoric and preaching, has preserved the vital sap, while breaking off with the affectedness of early romanticism's lyric tension, and a direct and, we should say, discursive rapport with the object.

Gorlier can well conclude, then, that "American literature is still greatly indebted to Thoreau, even as he is unfairly used or distorted" and that, while "Thoreau's archetypal character is at the root of the poetry of Wallace Stevens or William Carlos Williams," it is also true that "the 'national ego' of the American culture and the American individual bears his mark."

It is with Gorlier's book, then, that after the decades following World War II Italian studies of American literature are able to produce, both owing to the critic's individual merits and to a general high degree of maturity, a portrait of Thoreau which is indeed both complex and subtle. Such a portrait, however, is later enriched, in a human as well as a critical sense, by the 1963 translation of Emerson's *Journals*.[32] Here the Italian reader can view the relationship between the two men on a realistic and no longer legendary level; he is able to see Thoreau, through Emerson's eyes, in his daily life, his speeches, his actions, his habits and idiosyncrasies,[33] from his first encounters in 1838 with his "master" ("I delight much in my young friend, who seems to have as free and erect a mind as any I have ever met. . . . My good Henry Thoreau made this else solitary afternoon sunny with his simplicity and clear perception. How comic is simplicity in this double-dealing, quacking world. Everything that boy says makes merry with society, though nothing can be graver than his meaning") to the point when the encounters are already customary; from the moments of developing harmony ("The good river-god has taken the form of my valiant Henry Thoreau here and introduced me to the riches of his shadowy, starlit, moonlit stream. . . . Through one field only we went to the boat and then left all time, all science, all history, behind us, and entered into Nature with one stroke of the paddle") to those of bitter dissent ("Henry Thoreau sends me a paper with the old fault of unlimited contradiction. The trick of his rhetoric is soon learned: it consists in substituting for the obvious word and thought its diametrical antagonist . . . it makes me nervous and wretched to read it, with all its merits"); from the image, in 1856, of a Thoreau who is intent in his inexhaustible conversation with nature:

> Yesterday to the Sawmill Brook with Henry. He was in search of yellow violets which he waded into the water for; and which he concluded, on examination, had been out five days. Having found his flowers, he drew out of his breast pocket his diary and read the names of all the plants which should bloom this day, May 20; whereof he keeps account as a banker when his

32. R. W. Emerson, *Diario*, ed. and transl. by V. Amoruso (Venice 1963). Also in 1963 E. Zolla published his important essay on Transcendentalism (*Le Origini del Trascendentalismo*, Rome).
33. Useful to this purpose was also the appearance of N. Hawthorne, *Diario*, ed and transl. by A. Lombardo (Venice 1959).

notes fall due. . . . Then he heard a note which he calls that of the night-warbler, a bird he has never identified, has been in search of for twelve years, which, always, when he sees it, is in the act of diving down into a tree or bush, and which it is vain to seek; the only bird that sings indifferently by night and by day. I told him, he must beware of finding and booking him, lest life should have nothing more to show him. He said, "What you seek in vain for half your life, one day you come full upon—all the family at dinner. You seek him like a dream, and as soon as you find him, you become his prey." He thinks he could tell by the flowers what day of the month it is, within two days. . . . Water is the first gardener: he always plants grasses and flowers about his dwelling. There came Henry with music-book under his arm, to press flowers in; with telescope in his pocket, to see the birds, and microscope to count stamens; with a diary, jack-knife, and twine; in stout shoes, and strong grey trousers, ready to brave the shrub-oaks and smilax, and to climb the tree for a hawk's nest.

to a reminiscence of him, in 1862, shortly after his death:

Henry Thoreau remains erect, calm, self-subsistent, before me, and I read him not only truly in his Journal, but he is not long out of mind when I walk, and, as to-day, row upon the pond.

and to his opinion, in 1863, of Thoreau's journal:

In reading Henry Thoreau's journal, I am very sensible of the vigour of his constitution. That oaken strength which I noted whenever he walked, or worked, or surveyed wood-lots, the same unhesitating hand with which a field-labourer accosts a piece of work, which I should shun as a waste of strength, Henry shows in his literary task. He has muscle, and ventures on and performs feats which I am forced to decline. In reading him, I find the same thought, the same spirit that is in me, but he takes a step beyond, and illustrates by excellent images that which I should have conveyed in a sleepy generality. 'T is as if I went into a gymnasium, and saw youths leap, climb, and swing with a force unapproachable,—though their feats are only continuations of my initial grapplings and jumps.

But, of course, more important than the translations of Emerson's diary is Biancamaria Tedeschini Lalli's contemporaneous translation of an ample selection from Thoreau's *Journals*, with the title *Life of a Writer* (*Vita di uno Scrittore*).[34] It is a fine work, and a new, worthy example of the passionate interest this scholar has dedicated to Thoreau. Many sections, of course, had to be sacrificed, but still the selection was made with much intelligence and she succeeds in fully presenting the character of the book and of the author, thanks particularly to an Italian prose which knows how to unite philological and stylistic faithfulness. The translation, moreover, is preceded by both a bibliography which is among the most complete in existence and a long introduction in which the critic does not limit herself to merely rehashing material from her 1954 book but looks at the author with new eyes, utilizing the journals, also commented upon with extreme care, as a filter for individuating the total meaning—literary and human—of Thoreau, enlarging certain opinions while modifying others, acutely underlining certain aspects of Thoreau's sensibility such as his "availability to joy":

> . . . the psychological portrait of Thoreau which comes from his journals would be incomplete if an essential aspect were not understood: his personal availability to joy. . . . From its very first items the diary reveals this search of joy in reality. . . . The years fly past, the assertive tone, the self-confidence, the enthusiasm—they all grow thinner, arranging themselves into a more subdued and profound state of joy, but one which rejects tragedy as a profanation and an absurdity. . . .

or the "youthful stance" of the early Thoreau—the Thoreau of the first volumes of his diary and of *A Week* and *Walden*—with his "tendency to force the books to balance at any cost, to bend reality in order to fit his own ideals" and, on the other hand, "the shade of consciousness," the "sense of limits" to which the diary attests with the passing of time. Actually one of the major critical results which Professor Tedeschini Lalli achieves in her Introduction is the historical interpretation of Thoreau's career, the individuation of the passage—be it on a human level, a stylistic one, intellectual, or politi-

---

34. H. D. Thoreau, *Vita di uno Scrittore* (*I Diari*), ed. and transl. by B. M. Tedeschini Lalli (Venice 1963).

cal—from a "youthful" phase (which is, as *A Week* and *Walden* testify, not in the least non-creative) to a more mature phase which is principally expressed in the journals. Moreover, while correcting the perspective of her preceding monograph, she rightly enlarges the truly artistic experience of Thoreau from the autonomously published works to the journals, which are analyzed as a terrain of human and literary inquiry, a log of emotional and intellectual experience, and, above all, a finished work of art in which the writer fixes on the page, and transforms into myths, those data of reality which he has discovered and which now, at maturity, become "a great supply of fables out of which the poet must only draw with both hands full."

It seems fitting to conclude our brief history of Thoreau's "career" in Italy here; on one hand, the publication of the journals constitutes a point-of-arrival for all work—critical, expository, bibliographical—done in Italy on Thoreau (all of which is strongly reflected, moreover, at the university where Thoreau is among the authors most studied); on the other hand, the journals can act as a point-of-departure for a new phase of rapport between Thoreau and Italy, the phase, that is, in which the steady philological and critical investigation into this author may be joined by what has been until now too scarce a penetration into Italian literary culture. Poe and Whitman, Melville and Hawthorne, Emily Dickinson, Mark Twain —only to mention some major figures—have not only been objects of specialized studies but are a living part of our literary tradition which has absorbed and assimilated, with their works, their experience and language. This has not yet happened with Thoreau and the late date at which *Walden* was translated is convincing evidence of the fact. But now that his single works and a good part of his journals are available to the Italian reader and man of letters; now that the scholars and critics have done most of their job, transforming Emerson's faint shadow into a full-bodied figure and, above all, passing from the concept of Thoreau as a "naturalist" to the much truer concept of Thoreau as an artist, a writer *tout court* who uses the material he knows best in order to get at the truth; now, finally, that some of the aspirations of Thoreau the thinker can be so closely identified with some of the profound needs of modern man, the times are really ripe for Thoreau to become a part of that group of American classics to which we turn, as we always turn to classics, in order to draw a rich stylistic and intellectual lesson.

Thoreau's Influence in Bohemia

Otakar Vočadlo

OTAKAR VOCADLO is Professor of English Language and Literature at Caroline University in Prague. He has taught at Cambridge, London University, Komensky University and elsewhere. He founded English and American studies at Komensky University, Bratislava, and later, in Prague, he initiated American Studies as well as the first American Seminar in Central Europe. During World War II he was imprisoned in a concentration camp. His many publications include a book on modern English literature and another on modern American literature in addition to numerous studies on English and comparative lexicology. He is the editor of the first complete Czech translation of Shakespeare's works.

THOREAU'S INFLUENCE IN BOHEMIA

It is no exaggeration to say that the influence of American authors in Bohemia has been even stronger than that of British writers, the great trio of Shakespeare, Byron, and Scott excepted. Franklin was well known at the beginning of the nineteenth century, and a Czech anthology of Franklin's writings appeared in Slovakia in 1838. Irving's *Alhambra* fired the imagination of young Bozena Nemcová, the first important Czechoslovak woman novelist, who was also fond of Cooper's Leather-Stocking Tales. "The Gold Bug" was translated in 1853 and Poe's incantatory verse inspired even such popular modern poets as Bezruc and Nezval. Neruda, the classic story-teller of Prague, thought highly of Bret Harte's technique, and the art of *The Scarlet Letter* appealed to Masaryk himself, whose special favorite was, however, the author of *My Antonia*, Willa Cather. Mark Twain, who visited Bohemia during his travels and wrote an amusing account of its leading spa, left his mark on Czech juvenile literature. Otto's popular English Library started with *Tom Sawyer* and *Huckleberry Finn,* and the Aventinum Anglo-American Library has familiarized Czech readers with the best specimens of contemporary American prose.

Americans of Czech descent formed a link. Two Prague museums bear the names of prominent Czech Americans, V. Náprstek, an energetic interpreter of the American way of life, founded an ethnographic museum and A. Hrdlicka of the Smithsonian Institution an anthropological one. The first two lecturers in English at Prague University, J. V. Sládek, the translator of Shakespeare's plays, and V. A. Jung, the author of the standard Anglo-Czech dictionary, both received their training in the United States.

Reasons for the genuine kinship between the two peoples are clear enough. After the disastrous defeat of their revolution against the Hapsburg despotism, the Czechs lost their old aristocracy, and so, unlike their neighbors, the Hungarians and Poles, the Czechs emerged in modern times unencumbered by feudalism. Besides, their national character was deliberately molded by a band of democratic thinkers, especially K. Havlicek (whose statue stands in a Chicago park), and the world-wide Sokol gymnastic movement successfully obliterated undesirable class distinctions. It was only natural that the reborn state—created after the Washington Declaration of Czechoslovak Independence of 18 October 1918—should follow in all essentials the American pattern.

Thus the impact of Thoreau on representative Czech writers and critics is not particularly surprising. His reforming spirit is strangely congenial to the notorious heretic strain in the Bohemian character, a strain which seems to have survived all attempts at coercion. The great American moral teacher was bound to be appreciated among the people who from the times of John Hus produced a succession of remarkable moralists. Thoreau's gospel of individual freedom found an immediate response in the hearts of those who, like their hard-pressed ancestors, remained stubborn nonconformists. Instinctively, he shunned the blight of industrialism; and their protest against the leveling mechanism of modern life is best summed up in the term "robot" which Karel Capek's play has made international. Thoreau's secular, undogmatic turn of mind and his preference for Greek and Oriental thought were much to the taste of that section of Czech intelligentsia which, as often happens in countries long exposed to clerical domination, was distrustful of religious moralizing. In this respect Thoreau's philosophy, with its free examination of life's problems, proved more acceptable than the parallel influence of Tolstoy's Christian tracts. Besides, Tolstoy himself was impressed by Thoreau's thought. Some thirty quotations from his work are found in Tolstoy's *Circle of Reading*, which contains inspired passages from the world's outstanding thinkers and writers ranging from Buddha and Confucius down to his contemporaries, Henry George and A. P. Chekhov. Chekhov, too, was interested in Thoreau. In a letter to V. G. Korolenko (1887), a writer noted for his descriptions of Siberian nature, he drew his friend's attention to Thoreau's original ideas and freshness.

The influence of Thoreau the naturalist was equally powerful. Indeed, his intimate feeling for nature opened the eyes of millions of readers throughout the entire world. In this respect he resembles his celebrated Russian contemporary, Turgenev, whose artistic descriptions of animal and plant life were much admired in Bohemia. Another link between them was that social sensitivity which was revealed in their mutual antislavery sentiments.[1]

Pursuing a purely chronological order, we begin with one of Thoreau's earliest Czech admirers, the poet J. V. Sládek. During his travels in America he collected material for his sketch, *The First Century of American Literature* (Osveta, 1876). Two aspects of Thoreau's work seem to have particularly appealed to Sládek: Thoreau's natural descriptions and his sympathetic insight into Indian life and character. Sládek himself wrote with sympathy about the destiny of the American aborigines, and his translation of *Hiawatha* deeply influenced his countryman, Dvorák, when he was composing his celebrated *New World Symphony*. In his appraisal of Thoreau's work, Sládek stated that Thoreau penetrated into nature's heart deeper than any other American writer. His bird watcher friend, Professor Josef Thomayer, a medical man of repute and a nature lover who had written interesting descriptions of Bohemian ponds and meadows before Thoreau became known, was praised by Sládek as "the Bohemian Thoreau." Because Sládek was the editor of the leading literary journal of his day, such a sobriquet was of significance.

Professor Václav Mourek, the founder of English studies at Prague University, was the next to appreciate Thoreau's poetic sensibility as

---

1. The work of these two unromantic lovers of nature—both were bachelors—coincides. Turgenev started publishing his *Sportsman's Sketches*, an important literary contribution towards the abolition of serfdom, in 1847, the same year in which Thoreau began lecturing about his Walden experience, and their epoch-making books were both ready for the press at about the same time.

revealed in the essays on nature. He considered these to be among the best examples of English prose. In the standard Czech encyclopedia (*Ottuv Slovník Naucny*) he characterized Thoreau as an acute observer who, through his close union with nature, came to identify himself with the natural phenomena he described.

The starting point of Thoreau's direct influence was the publication of his masterpiece in 1902. The publisher who introduced him to Czech readers was Jan Laichter, an enlightened and self-made man, who has been the most outstanding figure in the history of the Czech book trade. His policy was to publish only serious books, and he made it a point to read every book he published. By attracting the best scholars of the day he was able to raise his house to a position higher than that of any other in the country. Since there was no university press in Prague, his firm filled the gap by publishing great cooperative and encyclopedic works on history, literature, politics, philosophy, economics, sociology, and art, written or edited by acknowledged university authorities. In recognition of his significant contribution to Czechoslovak scholarship and educational life, he was made an honorary doctor of philosophy by the Charles University in 1947.

From the beginning, his publishing career was linked closely with the pioneering activities of Professor T. G. Masaryk, the architect of Czechoslovak independence. For fifty-five years his firm sponsored Masaryk's important review, *Nase Doba* (*Our Time*). He also published Masaryk's chief works. For encouragement and direction Laichter owed much to Masaryk, whose personality and preference for English thought strongly appealed to Laichter. That Laichter's own interests were along these same lines is indicated by the fact that his favorite author was Thoreau, and he had all of Thoreau's works near at hand in his office. He liked the uncompromising, nature-loving, social thinker. This energetic man of business was also a lover of nature, and he found *Walden* to be a congenial companion. It was the first book in English that fell into his hands when he was studying the language, and he decided to publish it in a new series of stimulating books covering a variety of topics, *Problems and*

Opinions. He carefully chose the works himself; they included writings by such American thinkers as Thomas Paine, R. W. Emerson, Walt Whitman, Henry George, William James, George Santayana, John Dewey, and Stuart Chase. But Thoreau headed the list. In addition to works of fiction by American writers, e.g., Mark Twain, Sinclair Lewis, and Susan Glaspell, he published a manual of American literature by Trent and Erskine and an original Czech book on contemporary American literature by Otakar Vocadlo.

Of the various successful collections produced by the enterprising publisher none seems to have enjoyed greater popularity than that which was inaugurated at the beginning of the century by Thoreau's *Walden*, together with its stoic counterpart, Epictetus's *Enchiridion*. Thoreau's translator, Zdenek Franta, an inspector of high schools and a friend of both Masaryk and Laichter, shared their Anglo-American orientation. In the preface to his careful translation he expressed the hope that Thoreau's spiritual autobiography would evoke a powerful response in the hearts of his own Czech countrymen, an expectation that was fully justified by results. During World War II Franta, though his family was cruelly persecuted by the Gestapo, managed to prepare a revised edition of his translation. American books, however, were forbidden by German censorship. After the war the Laichter publishing firm prepared a new edition of *Walden*, illustrated by the well-known American artist of Czech descent, Rudolf Ruzicka, which was ready in the spring of 1949. Distribution, however, was suspended pending the nationalization of the Czechoslovak book industry. It was finally released by the state book selling center in 1951, and the entire edition was sold out in one week. Thus by a curious coincidence the book which heralded Laichter's successful earlier venture also provided the finale for his great publishing firm.

The widespread influence of *Walden* in Bohemia was, no doubt, partly due to the warm reception it received from influential Prague critics. To most of them it came as a revelation. Jan Voborník, a literary historian of repute who wrote for the leading Prague daily, dwelt on Thoreau's independent mind, his tendency to simplify, his optimism, and the lyrical charm of his descriptions of nature. Probably the most important and certainly the most enthusiastic reviewers were those associated with the university. Otakar Kádner, a professor of pedagogy and the author of a voluminous history of education, stressed Thoreau's knowledge of the classics and the educational value of the book. Vlastimil Kybal, a professor of history and the author of a standard work on John Hus, admired Thoreau's harmonious philosophy; he pointed out, also, his kinship with Tolstoy. He concluded with the declaration that he had not yet read any book that was so "natural, true, and holy." But of particular interest is the eloquent tribute of F. X. Salda, professor of modern literatures at Prague University and the leading Czech critic of his time. Salda, himself a master stylist, appreciated the metaphorical richness of Thoreau's poetic prose which was derived from his study of Sir Thomas Browne. His praise of Thoreau's genius amounts to a panegyric:

> The deeper you penetrate into this book the more you become aware of its purity and auroral freshness. The heavenly breath touching your cheeks makes you feel that this poet and philosopher has arrived from the *country of youth*—a country infinitely more youthful than his native country, America—a country where time had come to a standstill thousands of years ago, or rather where its stream had flowed by, so that as Thoreau so beautifully puts it, "eternity remains." So much beautiful, naive assurance, faith, honesty, and heroism does this man bring into our stale, outworn, skeptical, and weary world; and like all fairy tale heroes, the bringers of the water of life, he, too, carries his gift—simply and without formalities in his helmet, part of his everyday armor, his customary outfit—in his diary, relating sometimes in minutest detail his economy and way of life during his prolonged seclusion on the boundary between civilization and wilderness, culture and nature.

The conclusion of his essay deserves to be quoted in full:

> Thoreau pushes through stereotyped schemes and commonplaces, everything derivative and abstract, and the dead layer of tradition and past history to the very soil and bedrock of

life, to its dark, life-giving roots: he deepens the silted, shallow bed. He has an unerring sense of all basic and elementary needs of the human soul; indignantly he resents the tragedy of an artificial, imitative, and over-civilized age. During an epoch in which man is choking with dainty dishes, surfeited with sweetmeats, Thoreau points to healthy hunger and sings a hymn to brown bread won by the labor of one's own hands. This mystic is a philosophical realist: he has a tremendous, unswerving sense of *reality*, of *fact*, from the greatest fact, that of eternity, to the least, such as the tracks of a forest animal in snow or the color of an autumn leaf sticking upon a cobweb covered with dewdrops. Unperturbed by accumulated lies, frauds, and wiles, he goes straight towards reality. There is, therefore, in the ethical and social world no greater enemy of idols and bogies than Thoreau, whether they concern state or church, property and humdrum patriotism, fashionable and popular literature, or the press and a thousand other abominations which are "the glory of our time." With two or three jerks Thoreau pulls off their theatrical garb and points to the lifeless and unprofitable sticks and poles underneath (*Volné Smery* [*Free Trends*], VII [1903]).

Another admirer of Thoreau's ideas was Professor Arne Novák. A perceptive critic, Novák criticized the Danish novelist, J. V. Jensen, for omitting in his book on America any mention of the Concord transcendentalists. Further, he deplored the fact that Thoreau, who would have led us better than anyone else into the promised land of open air and free humanity, is remembered only as an exquisite painter of nature. On the occasion of the seventieth anniversary of Thoreau's death, in 1932, Novák paid an eloquent tribute to the American in *Lidové Noviny* (*People's News*). He emphasized that uniqueness of Thoreau's which eluded all attempts at literary classification, and he asserted that Thoreau brought a new message to the world: freedom of the heart in close union with nature and freedom of the spirit vis-à-vis the encroachment of government. In spite of his erudition in classical and modern literature and in philosophy, Novák wrote, Thoreau resembled a modern Diogenes, an American St. Francis. His valiant independence from external forces makes him an heroic figure, and he ranks high among the classic poetic naturalists.

Another translation of *Walden* was made available to Czech readers in 1924. It appeared in a collection of nature books, itself called *Walden*, which was edited by the new translator, Milos Seifert, and B. Z. Nekovarík. Emerson's funeral oration is included, preceded by an enthusiastic introduction in which Seifert deals with the relations between the two friends. He emphasizes Thoreau's manliness and wisdom, and he asserts that, far from being a romantic dreamer, Thoreau was a well-balanced, solitary thinker who lived in complete harmony with nature. This translation was reissued in 1933 by the well-known publishing house of Jan Otto.

Another book by Thoreau appeared in Laichter's series, *Problems and Opinions*, in 1925. It is a collection of thirteen essays entitled *Excursions and Glimpses into Society*. Nine were translated by Zdenek Franta, the rest by Cenek Kocí. The book, introduced by Emerson's biographical sketch, is divided into two parts. The first part contains the following essays: "Walking," "Autumnal Tints," "A Winter Walk," "Night and Moonlight," "May Days," and "Days and Nights in Concord." The second part has two fragments from Thoreau's letter to Blake, "Love," "Chastity and Sensuality," followed by "Civil Disobedience," "Life without Principle," "A Plea for Captain John Brown," "The Last Days of John Brown," and "After the Death of John Brown."

From Thoreau's first book, *A Week on the Concord and Merrimack Rivers*, only the passage on friendship starting with "Friendship is evanescent . . ." was put into Czech in 1927. Its translator, J. M. E. Leseticky, a lyric poet and disciple of Whitman who wrote under the pen-name of Emanuel z Lesehradu, also translated from Ruskin and Emerson, both of whose names were often linked with Thoreau's in the minds of his many Czech admirers.

Apart from the unanimous testimony of the best literary critics, Thoreau's masterpiece cast its spell on thousands of delighted readers who felt themselves attuned to him. His stimulating message of a simple life, together with his sane and practical idealism, came as a healthy tonic for all those who were dissatisfied with the complexities of industrial civilization. Among those who profited most by his teachings were a number of thwarted intellectuals, sick of unnatural town life, to whom he offered a way out. Seeking solitude "far from the madding crowd," they found in him a perfect companion. But *Walden* was also read avidly by the younger generation, especially the Boy Scouts eager for open-air pursuits, and, needless to say, Thoreau's affection for animals won for him devoted adherents among naturalists and humanitarians.

The blunt honesty of mind and courageous firmness with which Thoreau resisted what he considered wrong captivated philosophical-minded moralists and reformers. Three of them deserve to be singled out as genuine Thoreauists. They were persons of consequence: the first, Jaros, was a Prague government functionary and idealistic journalist; the second, Seifert, was an inspired educationist; and the third, Kovarík, was a prominent actor. Foremost among them was Gustav Jaros, who wrote under the pen-name of Gamma. During and after the first World War he distinguished himself as a writer on nature, art, and society who combined a Ruskinian love of beauty with the indignation of a fervent moralist and caustic critic of competitive society. Like H. S. Salt, Shaw's friend and Thoreau's first English biographer, Jaros was an ardent advocate of food reform. In this respect too he followed Thoreau who supported the dietetic system of Sylvester Graham,[2] the famous opponent of meat, sugar, and devitalized white bread. In his writings Jaros repeatedly alludes to Thoreau's noble example of voluntary poverty and abstention from luxury. In a thoughtful essay, "The Fruit and the Tree," included in a beautiful book entitled *Brázda* (*The Furrow*, 1917), the author does not hesitate to place Thoreau next to such great moral teachers and prophets of mankind as Socrates, Epictetus, Brother Gregory, and even Buddha and Jesus. In another essay in the same collection he developed the idea that Thoreau's memorable experiment on the shore of Walden Pond had amply demonstrated

---

2. In Czechoslovakia his name is associated with brown bread made of unbolted flour.

how little one needs for a full, rich, and happy life. In the second volume of essays called *Vánoce* (*Christmas*, 1920) Jaros recommended *Walden* as an ideal Christmas gift, a guide to the art of living. Although we cannot imitate Thoreau in every detail, he remarked, we should follow in his footsteps for as far as we can.

A new wave of interest in Thoreau's work came with the Scout and Woodcraft movements, the chief representative of which was Milos Seifert (1887–1941). Born at Susice on the fringe of the Bohemian Forest, he was introduced at an early age to the study of nature by his father, headmaster of the local high school. A grammar school teacher like Thoreau, Milos Seifert was far in advance of his time as a pioneer of new methods of open-air education. He founded the Woodcraft League and edited its organ, *Vatra* (*Bonfire*). He repeatedly expressed his indebtedness to Thoreau, whose ideas on woodcraft, Seifert claimed, were further developed by E. Thompson Seton. (Seton's books on wild animals were published in the *Walden* collection.) In addition to an introduction for his translation of *Walden*, he wrote a short book on Thoreau for juvenile readers, *H. D. Thoreau, Philosopher of Nature*, which came out under his Indian pen-name of Woowotanna. It was published by the Czechoslovak Red Cross in a collection, *Great Lives* (1934). The first part describes Thoreau's life; the second deals with *Walden*.[3] Like Thoreau, Seifert was regarded by some as an eccentric. He was unconventional in his dress as well as in his vegetarian diet, and he had the courage of his convictions. Also like Thoreau, he attracted an occasional disciple or admirer, one of whom was Dr. A. S. Batek, who gave up chemical research to become a teacher of ethics and a popular open-air lay preacher.

Another original follower of Thoreau was Frantisek Kovarík (b. 1886). In his philosophy of life and his career he probably comes the closest to Thoreau's principles of the three. When he was seventeen his uncle from South Dakota took him to America where he spent five years in a variety of occupations, among which were jour-

---

3. A biography of John Ruskin, whom he called an "apostle of truth and beauty," followed in 1937.

nalism and acting. From this process of trial and error, he discovered that his true vocation was in the theater, and he returned to Bohemia as an actor. During the first World War, however, his career was interrupted, for he was conscripted and employed as a factory worker. After the war he turned to nature for health and wisdom. For a time he lived in a riverside hut studying Emerson and other American writers. Later he led a gypsy life, roaming in South Bohemia and earning his living as a tinker. He slept in the woods, and occasionally he entertained village children with puppet shows. In 1920 he joined the Prague Municipal Theater.

For Kovarík, Thoreau was a revelation, a magic luminary which cast light, as he put it, on his life's path. He called him "the prince of woodcraft." His short essays, e.g., "At the Riverside in March," have a distinct Thoreauesque flavor. Like Thoreau and Seifert, Kovarík was fond of children; he wrote plays for them and contributed to children's magazines.

Under the German occupation all cultural institutions including Sokol, Scouts, and kindred freedom-loving movements were suppressed and their leaders sent to concentration camps, where most of them perished. One of the lamented victims was Jaroslav Simsa (1900–1945), who had been President Masaryk's librarian, secretary of the Prague Y.M.C.A., editor of its review, and translator of Santayana's essays. He died at Dachau two months before the camp was liberated by the Americans. Shortly before his death he managed to smuggle out of the camp a long letter to his children. It appeared after the war in Laichter's collection, *Problems and Opinions*, under the title "Christmas Reflections on Books." His list of best books for young readers shows his Anglo-American orientation. Besides Seifert's writings on woodcraft, he recommends *Hiawatha*, Eastman's *Red Indian Tales*, and the Walden collection of nature books.

In 1962 the Thoreau centenary passed unnoticed in Czechoslovakia. However, in 1966 a special Thoreau program, in which some leading Czech actors took part, was broadcast by the Prague Radio. It was arranged by Dr. Jaroslav Schejbal of the Palacky University.

He emphasized the unfading charm of Thoreau's personality, his wit, his hatred of war and slavery, and the conflict between his fearless spirit and the authorities on matters of conscience.

Looking back today, 150 years after Thoreau's birth, we may safely say that his deep influence, both direct and indirect, is beyond dispute. His poetic vision had immediate appeal to Czech men of letters, and his ethical intuition proved to have a beneficial influence on the young. It drew their attention to the enjoyment of nature and the value of the simple life, thereby bringing them relief from the tensions of the modern world while at the same time it helped to build their character. The sage of Concord, New England's parochial Athens, is not likely to be forgotten in Czechoslovakia.

Thoreau in Russia

Jerzy R. Krzyzanowski

JERZY R. KRZYZANOWSKI is Professor of Slavic Languages and Literatures at Ohio State University. He received his Ph. Magister in the history of Polish literature at the University of Warsaw, and his Ph.D. in Comparative Literature at the University of Michigan. He has taught at the universities of California (Berkeley), Michigan, Colorado, and Kansas. His study, *Ernest Hemingway*, came out in 1963, and a monographic study of Wladyslaw Stanislaw Reymont is soon to appear. He has published numerous articles and reviews in American, British, Canadian, and Polish journals.

THOREAU IN RUSSIA

On 15 October 1887 the leading Russian daily, *Novoe Vremya* (*New Times*), published the first installment of *Walden*, entitled simply "In the Forest." Although Thoreau's name must have been known earlier to at least a handful of Russian intellectuals, it actually was the first Russian publication of his work made available to the reading public, and the fact that it appeared in the well-established, conservative periodical carefully edited by A. S. Suvorin, whom D. S. Mirsky called in *A History of Russian Literature* "a shrewd and clever" man, added to its significance.

An immediate response came from Anton Chekhov, who did not fail to notice that important cultural event. Chekhov, who at that time was closely associated with Suvorin and who had become the feature writer in *Novoe Vremya*, reacted in a very characteristic manner, as an artist rather than somebody aware of the philosophical and social meaning of *Walden*. In a private letter dated 17 October 1887 he wrote to his personal and literary friend, Vladimir Korolenko:

> By the way, I am sending you a clipping from *Novoe Vremya*. That Thoreau, with whom you will get acquainted through it, I will clip out and keep for you.
> The first chapter is very promising; there are thoughts, there is freshness and originality, but it is hard to read. Its architecture and its construction are impossible. The beautiful and the plain thoughts, the light and the heavy ones are put one onto another, they are crowded, they squeeze lifeblood from each other and, after a while, they will choke from suffocation.
> When you arrive in Moscow I will hand that Thoreau over to you, and for now—so long and adieu.[1]

Chekhov's concern with problems of style could be well under-

---
1. A. Chekhov, *Pis'ma* (Moscow, 1948) XIII, p. 376.

stood. It was in 1887 that he abandoned his humorous stories and began to work on a long narrative "The Steppe" (1888) which marked a new period in his artistic development, the period of "serious" stories in which "there is an inner, symbolic action expressed by the subtextual play and dialogue of themes and counter-themes, motifs and counter-motifs, as in a musical work."[2] As Thomas Winner pointed out, it was a turning point in Chekhov's literary career, and he must have been very keenly aware of questions of style; hence his reaction to Thoreau, whose *Walden* must have appeared strange and often incomprehensible in an amateurish Russian translation.

On the other hand, it seems quite possible that the intense love for nature which runs through *Walden* as the main motif might have affected, to a certain extent, Chekhov's poetical narrative about "the steppe which has not been described for a long time . . . perhaps it will open the eyes of my contemporaries and will show them what riches, what treasure of beauty have yet remained untouched and how much space there still is for the Russian artist."[3] Leaving aside speculations about any possible literary influence, one may only state the fact that such topics and the poetical style employed to present them had been conspicuously absent from Chekhov's prose before 1887.

For the next seven years there was no evidence of interest in Thoreau in Russia until the name of the American writer attracted Leo Tolstoy's attention. Tolstoy, however, showed a different kind of interest in Thoreau's writing than that of his great contemporary. Having undergone his conversion in the early 1880's the novelist turned toward the problems of religion and society, devoting much of his time to the study of social and socialist movements in Western Europe. On 3 September 1894 he wrote to his friend V. Chertkov:

2. T. Winner, *Chekhov and His Prose* (New York, 1966) p. 46.
3. Letter to D. V. Grigorovich, 12 January 1888, quoted by Winner *op. cit.*, p. 45.

From England there is also good news. I have received an annual of a journal, *Labour Prophet*. Very good. I have marked there some items to be translated. The editor is John Trevor; his articles are good. There is a wonderful article "Thoreau." There is a book by Thoreau, "On Civil Disobedience." I have to order it.[4]

The article in question written by Trevor for *Labour Prophet*, an organ of "Labour Church" published in Manchester, must have stimulated Tolstoy to learn more about the American writer in the years to come. After having read Thoreau in the original he decided to use his writings for support of his own ideas and at the same time make them available to the Russian public. With his consent Chertkov began to work on a periodical publication printed in England but intended for domestic use, as had been the case with the most successful journal *Kolokol (The Bell)* edited by A. Herzen in the 1860's and widely circulated in Russia. When the first issue of *Svobodnoe slovo (Free Word)* appeared in 1898, edited by P. Biryukov and published by Chertkov in Purleigh, Essex, it contained among other articles the first Russian translation of "On Civil Disobedience." As Aylmer Maud recalled in his *Conversations with Tolstoy*, it was Tolstoy's choice and wish to introduce Thoreau in that collection to the Russian readers:

> In spite of the activities of the secret police which spies on his friends, exiles them, and confiscates their papers, works which have been recommended by Tolstoy usually come through in Russian translation. So it happened with two works about which we shall tell.
> An essay by Thoreau "On Civil Disobedience" Tolstoy selected as the best one from that writer's work.[5]

The publication of *Svobodnoe slovo* opened a brief period of Thoreau's popularity in Russia. In 1900 an abridged translation of *Walden* appeared in Moscow, entitled *Opyt uproshchenya zhizni:*

---

4. L. Tolstoy, *Polnoe sobranye sochinenij* (Moscow, 1928–58), LXXXVII, p. 287.
5. A. Maude, *Tolstoy and His Problems* (New York, 1904), p. 189.

U Valdenskovo ozera v Amerike (An Experiment in Simplified Life: At Walden Pond in America) followed by a full translation by P. Boulanger, *Valden, ili zhizn' v lesakh (Walden, or Life in the Woods* [Moscow, 1910]). That edition included also a short biographical sketch written by Emerson. In the meantime I. Nikashidze translated a selection of Thoreau's thoughts, publishing it in 1903 as *Filosofya estestvennoy zhizni (Philosophy of Natural Life)*. That booklet, a copy of which can be found in Tolstoy's library in Yasnaya Polyana, served Tolstoy as a source for his selection of famous quotations, *Krug chtenya (A Circle of Reading)*, published in 1904–8 and including many of Thoreau's thoughts and ideas. Tolstoy also used an English edition, *Every Day with Thoreau*, a copy of which is now being kept in Tolstoy's State Museum in Moscow.

Tolstoy's debt to Thoreau, he felt, was very personal. In a letter to Edward Garnett, written in 1900 in English, he admitted as much:

> Dear Sir: I thank you very much for your letter of June 6th. When I read it, it seemed to me impossible that I could send any message to the American people. But thinking it over at night, it came to me that if I had to address the American people, I should like to thank them for the great help I have received from their writers who flourished about the fifties. I would mention Garrison, Parker, Emerson, Ballou and Thoreau, not as the greatest but those who I think specially influenced me.[6]

The sincerity of that statement could be debated in the light of two facts: first, the comparison between Thoreau and Tolstoy which proved them to be more different than alike in basic philosophical principles, as C. A. Manning pointed out,[7] and secondly the repetition of the same names in almost every statement Tolstoy made on American literature. However, it is true that Tolstoy knew Thoreau's ideas fairly well and that he used them to illustrate and emphasize

---

6. Tolstoy, *op cit.*, LXXII, p. 396. Also quoted by W. Harding, *A Thoreau Handbook* (New York, 1959), p. 198.
7. "Thoreau and Tolstoy," *New England Quarterly*, XVI (June, 1943) pp. 234–244.

his own ideas. In a letter to his German correspondent, Eugen H. Schmitt, written in 1896, Tolstoy discussed the problems of disobedience to the government, and added: "Thoreau was the first one to say that, I think, some fifty years ago. At that time nobody paid any attention to his refusal and article—it seemed to be so strange. They explained it as eccentricity."[8]

Some four years later Tolstoy again used Thoreau as an example in an interesting parable when referring to the state of Russian agriculture. As A. Goldenweiser recorded under the date 12 July 1900, Tolstoy told him the following story:

> One should not introduce expensive and complicated equipment. You know, there was a famous American writer, Thoreau, who departed from urban life and began to earn his living with his own hands. When his friends began to tell him that he lived just a few hours away from a beautiful lake and never intended to go there, even if a trip by train would be only two dollars, Thoreau argued with them saying that he felt very well at home; but if he would ever have intended to go to the lake he would rather walk there since he would have to work four days in order to earn two dollars while a walk could take him only two days. Such an argument we employ often in our country when we want to start improving agriculture by way of introducing expensive and complicated equipment.[9]

Goldenweiser's recollections also throw an interesting light on an opinion of another famous Russian writer, Ivan Turgenev, and his attitude toward American letters. On 12 August 1906 Goldenweiser recorded the following statement made by Tolstoy in a casual conversation:

> Another time, talking about an outstanding pleiad of American writers, Channing, Parker, Emerson, Garrison, Thoreau, Lev Nikolaevich said:
> "By the way, it is generally assumed that England has great writers while America did not have any. I remember how Turgenev, who was a highly educated man, told me very seri-

9. A. B. Goldenweiser, *Vblizi Tolstovo* (Moscow, 1959), p. 75.
8. Tolstoy, *op. cit.*, LXIX, p. 165.

ously that there were no significant writers at all in America" (*sovsem ne bylo znachitel'nykh pisateley*)[10]

Without questioning Turgenev's seriousness and education, one may recall a different opinion he was supposed to express in a letter to William Dean Howells when, after reading *A Chance Acquaintance* he said he "should like to visit the country where there are girls like the heroine" of that novel.[11]

The last recorded opinion on Thoreau, made just six months before Tolstoy died, seems to verify the sincerity of the statement quoted above. V. Bulgakov, who carefully wrote down his conversation with the author of *War and Peace*, remembers one of them on 25 May 1910:

> In the evening he said that he had read a book, *Walden*, and as he did not like it before, so he does not like it now. "Purposely original, boastful, restless," said Lev Nikolaevich about Thoreau.[12]

That opinion seems to close a circle which had originated half a century before and resulted in a brief period of Russian interest in the American writer. Curiously enough, both great Russians expressed their criticism concerning Thoreau's style rather than his ideas which somehow did not find any serious response on their part.

After Tolstoy's death Thoreau was almost completely forgotten. One cannot consider as valid such brief notes as entries in various Russian general and literary encyclopedias, or an article published in 1916 in a periodical of the Moscow Vegetarian Society. After the Revolution of 1917 that oblivion went so far that those Soviet critics who have devoted considerable research to establishing evidence of Tolstoy's relationship to various literatures around the world did not even mention Thoreau. Such was the case with a voluminous publication *Literaturnoe Nasledstvo* (*Literary Heritage*) whose volumes XXXVII–XXXVIII (Moscow, 1939) have been entirely devoted

---

10. *Ibid.*, p. 190.
11. C. M. and R. Kirk, *William Dean Howells* (New York, 1962), p. 80.
12. V. Bulgakov, *L. N. Tolstoy v poslednii god evo zhizni* (Moscow, 1957), p. 261.

to Tolstoy and world literature, or with a study *O mirovom znachenii L. N. Tolstovo* (*On world-wide significance of L. N. Tolstoy*) by T. Motyleva who meticulously pointed out ties between Tolstoy and many American writers whose names could hardly be found in a history of American literature. It should be remarked, on the other hand, that even such a detailed study as *East-West Passage* by Dorothy Brewster did not mention Thoreau among those Americans whose work aroused interest in Russia, and thanks only to Walter Harding some information has been made available to the growing number of Thoreau scholars in the United States.

In view of those facts a new Russian publication of *Walden* should be considered a major event of Thoreau's reception in Russia. *Uolden, ili zhizn' v lesakh*, with an English counter-title *Walden or Life in the Woods*, was published in 1962 by the Soviet Academy of Sciences in a series of "Literary Portraits." Among the members of the editorial board there are several names of the members of the Academy who are well-known beyond the boundaries of the Soviet Union, e.g., V. Vinogradov, D. Blagoy and V. Zhirmunsky. *Walden*, edited by Z. Alexandrova, A. Starstev, and A. Elistratova, is carefully translated and edited with explanatory notes and an afterword by Starstev, in 12,000 copies. The publication contains also a picture of Thoreau and a view of Walden Pond.

As is customary in that type of Russian publication, the afterword contains an ideological and historical introduction and explanation of the period as well as of *Walden* itself. A special emphasis has been put on its social significance as seen against the broad background of social movements in the United States in the 1840's. There is even a short chapter devoted to Thoreau's reception in the United States, but again, a conspicuous silence about his relationship to Russian literature. In spite of these omissions Starstev's essay is quiet in tone, objective, and full of genuine admiration for the artistic qualities of *Walden*. Those qualities, to be sure, are always seen in a specific light, namely with an emphasis on their social usefulness, since that is the accepted procedure in Russian criticism. Nevertheless, even with such a limited approach Starstev manages to underscore Thoreau's role as an artist, stressing his style and irony. He also mentions in passing an interesting similarity of images used by Thoreau in his famous description of a railroad, and those in a poem by N. Nekrasov "Zheleznaya doroga" ("Railroad").

And indeed, a brief comparison with the Russian poem, written in 1864 by the most outspoken of Russia's "civic poets" discloses a remarkable kinship in artistic devices used by both writers to express their anger with the cruelty of inhuman conditions and treatment of railroad workers who were to pay with their lives for the comfort of the future passengers. While Thoreau's image of dead bodies lying under the rails were figurative, Nekrasov's vision of the dead workmen changed into ghosts haunting the occupants of a luxurious railroad car was more imaginative.

> The road is straight. There are narrow embankments,
> And little poles, and rails, and bridges.
> But on the sides there are Russian bones...
> How many of them, do you know, Vanya?
>
> Hark! You can hear fierce shouts,
> A stamping and gnashing of their teeth.
> A shadow covered frozen windows.
> What is there? A crowd of the dead ones![13]

Nekrasov died in 1878, long before the first translation of *Walden* ever appeared in Russia. Nonetheless that striking similarity in an artistic presentation of the questions of social injustice may explain what the Russians actually have found in Thoreau, and what aspects of his writing appeal to them more than his philosophy and style. Always acutely aware and sensible to the social problems, the Russians apprehend only one of Thoreau's many facets, that which they have labeled "progressive" in its limited sense of social usefulness, and they almost completely disregard his philosophical and artistic endeavors; yet one can hope that the country of Chekhov and Tolstoy, whose names have been so strangely associated with the lonely inhabitant of Walden, will one day discover the real Thoreau.

13. N. Nekrasov, *Sobranye stikhotvorenij* (Leningrad, 1949), I, p 309.

Thoreau and Israel

Sholom J. Kahn

SHOLOM J. KAHN is senior lecturer in American literature at The Hebrew University of Jerusalem. He introduced the first courses in American literature at that university, and he has been living in Jerusalem and teaching there since 1950. His doctor's degree from Columbia University is in philosophy. He has published many articles on English and American literature, as well as on literary criticism and aesthetics; in addition, he has made many translations from the modern Hebrew poets. His chief areas of research are in Whitman, Melville, and Mark Twain with regard to writers; regarding subjects, he is concerned with the theory of criticism, with special application to the Search for Myth in American literature. As translator and critic, he has dealt largely with the interrelationships between literatures in Hebrew and English.

THOREAU AND ISRAEL

The problem of Thoreau and Israel presents a curious mixture of facts and possibilities. At first blush, Israel would seem to offer a fertile soil for Thoreauvian principles; in fact, however, his works seem to be little known or read. Yet the lover of Thoreau will feel that his spirit is to be felt on every hand, in some general manifestations and in many out-of-the-way corners of the land. (I am reminded of a remark made about my choice of pioneering and frontier life as the theme of a book designed to introduce American literature to the Israeli reader. "No one thinks or talks much about pioneering here," I was told; "the subject is not an attractive one." "Why not?" I asked. "It's too commonplace: where everyone *is* in some measure a pioneer, is living a daily pioneering existence, there is little point in making a fuss about it; people want something different.") One must therefore first describe, and account for, the pervasive ignorance; but one must also go on to explore some of the affinities of situation and spirit which may encourage more readers in the future. Thoreau is very definitely *in* Israel, in the sense that Whitman intended when he wrote: "If you want me again, look for me under your boot-soles."

I

Thoreau's writings were made available in Hebrew in 1962: *Walden* and "Civil Disobedience," in one volume (Bialik Institute, Jerusalem), translated respectively by Reuven Avinoam and Hanoch Kal'ai, with illustrations by Louise Schatz and an excellent introduction by Simon Halkin, Professor of Modern Hebrew Literature at The Hebrew University. Until then he was known, for the most part, as the author of an "anarchistic" pamphlet which had had an influence on Gandhi's work in India. As one example, we may cite the late Martin Buber, who wrote the following letter (the original is in German), on the occasion of Thoreau's centenary, for publication in *The Massachusetts Review* (Autumn, 1962):

> It is now nearly sixty years since I first got to know Thoreau's essay "Civil Disobedience." I read it with the strong feeling that here was something that concerned me directly. Not till very much later, however, did I understand the origin of this feeling. It was the concrete, the personal element, the "here and now" of this work that won me over. Thoreau did not put forth a general proposition as such; he described and established his attitude in a specific historical-biographic situation. He addressed his reader within the very sphere of this situation common to both of them in such a way that the reader not only discovered why Thoreau acted as he did at that time but also that the reader—assuming him of course to be honest and dispassionate—would have to act in just such a way whenever the proper occasion arose, provided he was seriously engaged in fulfilling his existence as a human being.
>
> The question here is not just about one of the numerous individual cases in the struggle between a truth powerless to act and a power that has become the enemy of truth. It is really a question of the absolutely concrete demonstration of the point at which this struggle at any moment becomes man's duty *as man*. By speaking as concretely as he does about his own historical situation, Thoreau expresses exactly that which is valid for all human history.
>
> Jerusalem, 15 October 1962

There is no mention of *Walden* or the journals here; but in a conversation with W. Stephen Thomas (reported in *The Thoreau Society Bulletin*, LXXXV [Fall, 1963]), Buber also remembered reading "Life Without Principle," and said, "Now, today, we are in an utterly different situation than Thoreau and we need an application of his principles."

Buber's reading of Thoreau at the turn of the century cannot be understood as an Israeli phenomenon, however, though it was part of the spiritual ambience out of which came one mainstream of

Zionism. Where East European Jewry was concerned, Thoreau does not seem to have been a serious influence; as recently as 1961, in a four-volume Hebrew encyclopedia designed to cover "general literature," his name did not appear at all. In Western Europe, however, Jewish readers encountered Thoreau because of his vogue in Germany. A striking instance—as far as I know, the only important one until 1962—was an excellent essay by "Rabbi Benjamin," pen-name of Joshua Radler-Feldman (b. 1880), who was also one of the first to introduce Whitman to Hebrew readers.[1] A native of Galicia, he spent some years in Berlin before coming to Palestine in 1908, where he wrote and lectured and became an influential figure as an editor. His "Thoreau" was included in the two-volume *Portraits* (*Partsufim* [Tel-Aviv, 1934]), a collection which opens with Marcus Aurelius and includes essays on Anatole France, Thomas Mann, and Booker T. Washington. Rabbi Benjamin did translations of essays by Emerson, and he used Emerson's eulogy to good advantage, opening with his well-known view of Thoreau as a stoic and linking Thoreau with Aurelius. He also quoted a description by Gorky of the aging Tolstoy in a moment of meditation, and compared it with Emerson on Thoreau: "He knew how to sit immovable, a part of the rock he rested on, until the bird, the reptile, the fish, which had retired from him, should come back and resume its habits, nay, moved by curiosity, should come to him and watch him." He went at length into the chapter of *Walden* on solitude; cited parallel ideas out of the Jewish rabbinic tradition; and ended by quoting Thoreau's parable beginning "I long ago lost a hound, a bay horse and a turtle-dove. . . ." Rabbi Benjamin also wrote on a number of occasions about Gandhi and his philosophy, but without mentioning Thoreau's influence, as far as I have read. Selections from *Walden* were included in English textbooks for the schools (1952) and universities (1954); the same Avinoam who later translated *Walden*, born in the States, included four translated

---

1. See *Walt Whitman Abroad*, ed. Gay Wilson Allen (Syracuse, 1955), p. 235.

Hebrew reader; but from my limited experience, it has not had many takers, at least to judge from what has appeared in print. When taught to university students, in English or in Hebrew, however, he has been popular and has spoken to their condition.[2] One wrote that she found his principles "identical with my own thoughts," especially concerning the growing hunger for superfluous luxuries in Israel. And another: "When a few days ago the newspapers were writing about the possibility of landing on the moon, I thought of Thoreau's being against the introduction of trains. It sounds childish not to use the train, but maybe the brain which invented the train has also thrown bombs over Jerusalem." Such comments, of course, relate only to Thoreau as purveyor of practical wisdom; they do not display much sophistication about his literary art, or even about what he meant. (He was not, for example, "against the introduction of trains.")

The general picture, in sum, is not one of great popularity and interest, though a potential seems to be there, judging from the reaction of university students. From the German idealist tradition, from writers and scholars of American origin, and from the influence of the schools and universities, some awareness seems already to have filtered through. The basic explanation for the present situation, as Dr. Johnson once phrased it when challenged about some point involving knowledge of a horse's anatomy, is probably "ignorance, sheer ignorance."

II

But the spirit of Thoreau, his ideas and problems and values? You find them everywhere. Perhaps the Israelis can dispense with

2. Quotations from students are made, with slight stylistic revisions, from papers submitted to Professor Irving Halperin (San Francisco State College) during 1964–65, when he was visiting professor, teaching Thoreau at The Hebrew University (Jerusalem) and at Haifa University College.

the American writer because they have so many "Thoreaus" of their own!

One tends to think of Israel as a collectivist society, and to set up a dichotomy between the group and the individual. But the old-young country has had many strong individualists who have approximated Thoreauvian principles. Most important was Aaron David Gordon (1856–1922), from Poland, who came to Palestine in 1904 and spent the last ten years of his life in the Galilean kibbutz, Degania (Grain of God), where he worked and lived and wrote. He was a saint-like but earthy figure, and his disciples became known as "Gordonites"; they have published and studied his works and tried to live up to his ideals—as have the followers of Thoreau with his works and ideals.

A volume of Gordon's *Selected Essays* was translated by Frances Burnce (New York, 1938), with sections devoted to "Labor," "Matter and Spirit," and "Man and Nature." Gordon was no poet, not even in Emerson's sense, much less in the sense that Thoreau was when he created in a masterwork the myth he had lived. He was something of a philosopher, or a preacher and teacher, or a spiritual leader and father. He was an original thinker, but some of his ideas, like those of many of his generation, derived from such writers as Nietzsche, the older Tolstoy, and the same Berdichevsky (Ben-Gurion) who was the father of one of our reviewers. Although he preached nationalism and social life within the community, he did share with Thoreau (although I believe he never read him) interests in Buddhism and vegetarianism; and his attitude towards the Arab was not unlike Thoreau's feeling for the American Indian.

One of the clichés of criticism of life in Israel today—comparable to similar criticisms in the States—is that the ideals of Gordon, and the generation of pioneers more generally, are being forgotten. The pastoral phase, if one may call it that, was much shorter in Palestine than in the States, and it has encountered the machine in both countries. The auto, refrigerator, washing-machine—and now, alas, in Israel too, the television set—have come to stay. The once young and primitive kibbutz settlements have become comfortable, prosperous, almost suburban. But new frontiers have come to replace the old, and certain old values remain, however embattled. I shall conclude by citing a few of these.

Two terms, perhaps, might best characterize Thoreau: The Walker, and The Seeker. Both activities are still strong in Israel. Despite the increasing encroachments of autos, Israelis still like to walk, and many still make something of a cult out of it. There is the annual mass hike, in the spring, which is a sort of secular pilgrimage to Jerusalem; but that's a highly organized affair, unlike Thoreau's solitary rambles. I have in mind, rather, certain small groups of habitual hikers, who love to explore the countryside—forsaken wadis, abandoned ruins, and archaeological sites. They even have a special Hebrew term for their activity: "leshotet"—to ramble.

And despite an increasingly competitive and materialistic economy and society, there are still very many groups engaged in spiritual search. That is probably the chief contrast here to Thoreau himself (but not to modern Thoreau societies!)—the need to engage in the search together, in groups, not as lone individuals. Eliezer Whartman has recently described one such group in *Conservative Judaism*.[3] Significantly, at the opening meeting in 1962, almost half came from kibbutzim, some were English-speaking, and there were sabras (native sons) as well as their veteran parents. One of their "retreats" was devoted to "Defining Ourselves."

The last word may be given to one of these Seekers, Yitzhak Maor, the possessor of two doctorates, whose father and grandfather were hassidic rabbis, a man in his sixties who chooses to live in a kibbutz:

> We are like A. D. Gordon, who remarked to Joseph Brenner: "I love the religion of my people in my innermost soul, even though I do not observe its traditions and am not religious

3. "Mevakshei Derekh: Seeking a Path," XIX (Winter, 1965), 49–58.

in the accepted sense of the term." He possessed a spiritual rather than a dogmatic point of view.

I respect the Orthodox, for had they not preserved *their* path, we would not be seeking *ours* today. But I cannot accept the concept of Torah from Sinai as do the Orthodox; I respect their right to their belief, and I expect them to accept my right to mine. Mine stems from the conviction that the Source of all things is invested with holiness and we are enjoined to share in that spirituality. . . . We must begin with ourselves, as individuals. We must be exemplars.

We may be asked: "Why have you created this association? Is it not enough that each does what is right in his own sight?" To this I reply: "We have banded together to break down the walls of isolation between us. We are encouraged to know that others seek the same path. Ours is not to complete the task— but neither are we free to desist from it."

Though this is not precisely Thoreau's doctrine, he would have understood its language well.[4] It may be objected that in the 1960's the serious Seekers in Israel are not typical, have become an ineffectual minority. But when have Thoreauvians ever been a majority in the States? When they become such, in both countries, we shall be approaching the days of the Messiah.

4. Since the foregoing was completed, I have also written "Thoreau and Whitman in Israel," a paper for discussion at a seminar on "Asian Response to American Literature" (Srinagar, 1–7 June 1970), sponsored by U.S.E.F.I. (New Delhi, India).

Thoreau in India

Sujit Mukherjee

SUJIT MUKHERJEE has for the past several years been on the faculty of the Department of English at the University of Poona. His doctoral degree is from the University of Pennsylvania. He is the author of *Passage to America: The Reception of Rabindranath Tagore in the United States, 1912–1941* (Calcutta, 1964) and joint editor of *Indian Essays in American Literature* (Bombay, 1968), a Festschrift for Robert E. Spiller. He has written numerous articles, and his translations of modern Bengali poetry have appeared in a number of journals. Although he is still connected with academic life as a member of the editorial board of *Indian Journal of American Studies*, he is now with the publishing firm of Orient Longmans.

THOREAU IN INDIA

When Mohandas Karamchand Gandhi and Martin Luther King meet, as they very likely have by now, they are bound to compare notes on Thoreau and civil disobedience. No record, alas, will be kept of this conversation, no handbook of revolution will emerge, no published evidence ever be available to doctoral dissertation writers of the future. But those of us who occasionally become aware that we lead lives of quiet desperation cannot but be grateful that these three persons of three different races and three different times have demonstrated by what they learned from each other that mankind is essentially one.

It is generally accepted that by virtue of the impression he made on the mind of Mahatma Gandhi, Thoreau has had a share in the making of modern India. Thoreau's own interest in India will be obvious to the reader of his journals or *A Week on the Concord and Merrimack Rivers* or *Walden*. When an Indian reads lines like "Beside the vast and cosmogonal philosophy of the *Bhagvad Geeta*, even our Shakespeare seems sometimes youthfully green and practical merely," or "It seems to have been uttered from some eastern summit, with a sober morning prescience in the dawn of time, and you cannot read a sentence without being elevated as upon the tableland of the Ghauts," or "I lay down the book and go to my well for water, and lo! there I meet the servant of the Bramin, priest of Brahma and Vishnu and Indra, who still sits in his temple on the Ganges reading the Vedas . . .," he is filled with that sense of gratification which unexpected approbation from abroad always brings. But it is a much more dramatic experience to know the story of how

---

I am indebted to the American Studies Research Centre, Hyderabad (India), and especially to its Director, Dr. William Mulder, for making available much information and material that would have been unobtainable anywhere else in the country.

Gandhi read Thoreau's essay "The Duty of Civil Disobedience" while in a jail in Pretoria in 1907, and became aware of the connection with Gandhi's own *satyagraha* movement which was launched some fourteen years later. Yet another act of this drama was unfolded in the southern states of America under the stage directions of the Reverend King.[1] This passage of an idea to and from India and America is remarkable enough as an incident in recent world history, but at the moment it tends to rule out any other consideration of Thoreau's impact upon India, a country which had given him—to say the least—so much reading material. It is easy and modish to foist a thesis upon a seeming affinity between minds. For example, Jawaharlal Nehru's *The Discovery of India* ends with a quotation from Emerson; India's discovery of Nehru terminated, in a way, with a quotation from Robert Frost. Shall we therefore weave a pattern of influences to contain these personalities? The Thoreau-Gandhi entente has already become a straw for Indo-American amity for both nations to clutch at on appropriate occasions. The Thoreau Centennial provided such an occasion in 1962, and the Indian Ambassador to the United States made a whole log out of this straw when he delivered his address[2] at the dedication of Malvina Hoffman's bust of Thoreau in the Hall of Fame at New York University. The Gandhi Centenary celebrations in 1969 will create more such occasions for stately reminders of how much Gandhi owed to Thoreau and what Thoreau owed to India. The question we have to ask ourselves here, however, is—has Thoreau mattered to Indians other than Gandhi?

Where should one look for the answer to this question? On the one hand, we know that extracts from *Walden* have appeared in one form or another in school textbooks of English all over India

---

1. In his introduction to a paperback edition of *Satyagraha*, King wrote of Gandhi's influence upon his own belief in non-violence.
2. "Thoreau the Nonconformist," reproduced in *Thoreau and India* (*American Review* Supplement: October 1962). Reprinted as "Henry David Thoreau: A Tribute," *The Thoreau Centennial*, ed. Walter Harding (State University of New York Press, 1964), pp. 112–119.

for a long time; and those who have got through college would scarcely have done so without also having read "Civil Disobedience." The Sahitya Akademi (India's state-sponsored National Academy of Letters) launched a project in 1962 to translate *Walden* into all the regional languages of India; seven of these translations (in Bengali, Gujarati, Hindi, Kannada, Malayalam, Punjabi and Urdu) are already in print. Even without prompting and assistance from the government, *Walden* was translated into Malayalam in 1955, into Tamil in 1956, into Telugu in 1958. In Marathi, a language of western India, it is possible to read *Five Essays and Six Excerpts from Thoreau's Correspondence* (1957) and *Thoreau's Selected Writings on Nature and Liberty* (1961), besides parts of *Walden* (1957) and a complete translation which appeared in 1966. Yet another selection of Thoreau's writings is available in Gujarati, published in 1961. The first Indian reprint of *Walden* came out during 1962, though financed by the United States Information Service in India and carrying a preface by an American professor. Subsequently, USIS has also made possible an Indian reprint of *A Week* (1967), and this has an introduction written by an Indian scholar. I offer these bibliographical references to show that Thoreau's writings, in the original and in translation, are available at present in India on a scale unmatched by the works of any other major American author. So when the Indo-Anglian novelist P. M. Nityanandan begins a chapter of his *The Long Long Days* (1960), a novel of college life in southern India, with the statement, "It has long been recognized that man cannot live long in peaceful seclusion, except for a few rugged individualists like Thoreau" (p. 37), he seems to be banking on a common knowledge among Indian readers of who Thoreau was and what he stood for.

For evidence on the other side of the case, it is easy to find fairly recent records of American dismay at Indian ignorance of American literature. Professor Frederick Ives Carpenter, an Emerson scholar and hence already inducted into Indo-American thinking, found on his trip to India in 1961 that "if the influence of the American transcendentalists upon the greatest political leader and thinker of modern India was both spectacular and significant, their influence upon modern Indian scholars and university students has been much less important."[3] A great-grandson of Nathaniel Hawthorne and his successor as a distinguished American consulate officer abroad wrote in 1962: "What American writers do Indians know? Half a dozen in the nineteenth century: Hawthorne and Longfellow, Emerson and Thoreau, Whitman—that about covers the list. . . . What Indians know of nineteenth century American writers, they know from their study of classic writers of English literature in school—just as American and English schoolboys know them."[4] And John T. Reid was encouraged, he says, to make his preliminary survey of India in American writings by the feeling that "Many Indian students are aware of the remarkable impact that Indian philosophical literature had in the nineteenth century on the English Romantics, German authors and philosophers and some of the French literary men. It has been less commonly known to them that many Americans received the Indian scriptures with no less interest."[5] These observations are particularly applicable to Indian interest in Thoreau, as may be illustrated from the curious coincidence that the first three Indian publications specifically devoted to American literature—namely, *Literary Criterion*, VI (Summer 1964—Essays on American Literature); *Osmania Journal of English Studies*, V (1966—American Literature Number); *Indian Response to American Literature*, ed. C. D. Narasimhaiah (New Delhi, 1967)—not one carries an essay on Thoreau.[6]

In trying to explain this relative neglect of the older American authors in India, Carpenter has suggested that as a result of the

---

3. "American Transcendentalism in India," (1961), *Emerson Society Quarterly*, No. 31 (2nd. Quarter, Part II, 1963), pp. 59–60.
4. Manning Hawthorne, in preface to a volume edited by him, *American Literary Scene* (Bombay, 1962), p. v.
5. Preface, *Indian Influences in American Literature and Thought* (New Delhi, 1965), p. vi.
6. Two recent volumes, *Indian Essays in American Literature* (Bombay, 1968) and *The Experience of American Literature* (Delhi, 1969), carry papers on Thoreau.

long British rule of India, British authors had held the stage of Indian reading up to 1947 to the exclusion of all other foreign authors, even to the extent of American books not being readily available in public libraries (p. 60). This explanation cannot really be accepted at face value, because book-banning was never among the major preoccupations of the British Raj. The only books to be proscribed during British rule were those which criticized the regime, especially those written by Indians. From the kind of reading our fathers and grandfathers appear to have done, it is difficult to imagine that they were unaware of or were denied access to significant writing from anywhere in the world. To make a sampling of Thoreau alone, the 1917 Catalogue of the library of the Bombay branch of the Royal Asiatic Society lists an 1865 edition of *Cape Cod*, an 1884 *Walden*, and a volume entitled *Anti-slavery and Reform Papers*—(1890)—all, of course, London editions.

Two of the three Indian publications on American literature mentioned above include substantial essays by Indian scholars on Emerson; the Royal Asiatic library owned in 1917 the six-volume *Works* (1883–84) and the ten-volume *Journals* (1904–14) besides four other Emerson titles, as against only four volumes of Thoreau. Thoreau may have stood clear of Emerson long ago in America, but in India he continues to dwell in the lengthening shadow of Emerson. Although Emerson's subtle doubter-and-the-doubt is almost a contemporary of Thoreau's artist of Kouroo, Emerson had come much earlier to Indian thought, and Indians have requited by a longer history of interest in Emersonian thought. Soon after Protap Chunder Mazoomdar visited America in 1883 to lecture at the Concord School of Philosophy,[7] he contributed a paper entitled "Emerson as Seen from India" to the volume *The Genius and Character of Emerson* (Boston, 1885). In looking through back numbers of the *Harvard Theological Review*, one comes across the article by Herambachandra Maitra, "Emerson from an Indian Point of View,"

---

7. See Arthur Christy, "Orientalism in New England: Whittier," *American Literature*, I (1929–30), pp. 372–392.

in the October 1911 issue. When Rabindranath Tagore spoke at the University of Chicago in 1913, Edwin Herbert Lewis felt that it was like listening to a speech by Emerson.[8] All three of these Indians were associated with the Brahmo Samaj movement, that courageous attempt to reform Hinduism and return it to its monotheistic origins. This movement found many of its principles embedded in the Unitarian thought of Emerson, thereby laying the foundations of Indian respect for Emerson, even outside the circumscribed constituency of school and college textbooks. We may conjecture, therefore, that Emerson has been absorbed by the mainstream of sociocultural thought in India while Thoreau has been only a factor of political action. In fashioning a political sword out of the ploughshare of only one aspect of Thoreau's thinking, Gandhi thrust Thoreau into a context from which it is difficult to dislodge him.

And even Gandhi seems to have been as responsive to Emerson as he was to Thoreau. Extracts from both were reproduced from time to time by Gandhi in the columns of his South African newspaper, *Indian Opinion*.[9] Gandhi's phrase about "Indian wisdom in a western guru," in a letter to his son from South Africa in March 1909, refers to Emerson's essays. In the same letter[10] Gandhi wrote that Emerson, Ruskin and Mazzini "confirm the view that education does not mean a knowledge of letters but it means character building." This galaxy of educators and character-builders included—as far as Gandhi was concerned—Tolstoy, whose *Letter to a Hindu* (1908), had reached Gandhi in jail in South Africa not long after "The Duty of Civil Disobedience" had arrived there. When writing an introduction to the first edition of *Indian Home Rule* (1910),[11]

8. Cited by Tagore's Bengali biographer, Prabhatkumar Mukhopadhyay, in *Rabindra-jibani*, 4 vols. (Calcutta, 1945–56), II, p. 338.
9. For example, issues of 18 February 1905 ("The Over Soul") and of 26 October 1907 ("Civil Disobedience").
10. Quoted in Louis Fischer, *The Life of Mahatma Gandhi* (London, 1951), pp. 106–109.
11. This was originally written in Gujarati and entitled *Hind Swaraj*; the English translation first appeared serially in *Indian Opinion*. When published in book form, it was proscribed by the Bombay government. The

Gandhi paid tribute to the radical ideas of Emerson and Ruskin, Thoreau and Tolstoy, making it clear that more than the waters of Walden Pond had mingled with the Ganga (or the Sabarmati)[12] of Gandhi's enterprise. His concept of *satyagraha* was as much an answer to Tolstoy's overwhelming question, *What Then Must We Do?* (1885), as it was a response to Thoreau's directive to disobey. Dwelling on this theme in his address to the Tolstoy Death Anniversary Seminar at New Delhi in 1960, Prof. K. R. S. Iyengar proposed that "Thoreauistic civil disobedience and Tolstoyan passive resistance fused into the Gandhian dynamics of satyagraha."[13] Neither Tolstoy nor Thoreau, it must be remembered, went to the extent that Gandhi did in pitting his own convictions against the law of the land. And Gandhi did not really have to find his models so far from home as a village in America or a farm in Russia. As was recently pointed out to me,[14] the archetype of all civil disobedients in world history is the Indian prince, Prahlad, who refused to acknowledge the authority of King Hiranyakashypu, in a legend narrated in *Bhagavata-Purana*.[15]

Thoreau spent only one night in jail, and Gandhi read many more things besides Thoreau's essay before formulating his celebrated course of action. But "Civil Disobedience" remains instilled forever in Indian minds—or will remain, at least as long as Gandhi is remembered. Gandhi freely recommended the essay to friends and relatives, and his writings, especially between 1907 and 1921, contain numerous references to Thoreau.[16] He apparently carried "Civil

---

preface may be found in *The Collected Works of Mahatma Gandhi* (Publications Division, Govt. of India) X, pp. 188–190.
12. A river in Gandhi's home state of Gujarat, on the bank of which he set up his self-service community and social-service training camp, Sabarmati Ashram.
13. "Thoreau, Tolstoy and Gandhi," *Adventures in Criticism* (Bombay, 1964), p. 441.
14. By Prof. S. Ramaswamy, who remembers having seen *satyagraha* in action; retired Chief Professor of English, Presidency College, Madras.
15. No translation of this text was available in Thoreau's life-time.
16. Volumes VII to XIX of the *Collected Works* contain over twenty allusions to Thoreau.

Disobedience" to jail every time he was sent there, and even took it along with him to the Round Table Conference of 1931 in London.[17] Like his salt-making and his hand-spinning, this too was a symbol to be shared by the multitude and magnified by the sharing.

It is not surprising that it should be "Civil Disobedience" rather than *Walden* or any other of Thoreau's writings that has seemed significant to Indians. We read of the Walden experiment in school and immediately recognize what appears to be a kindred spirit in Thoreau, as I suppose young boys all over the world have done. Some of us may even discern—as I remember doing—a behavior pattern consisting of versions of "lighting out for the territory" which Americans such as Hawkeye and Huck Finn and Ishmael excitingly illustrated. The pattern became clearer for a time as I graduated in my reading of American literature to stories about Red Indians and cowboys. There is, of course, a special reason in India for accepting the *Walden* Thoreau as a familiar creature, so familiar that he does not engage our imagination thereafter. We may have neglected to practice it, but we are told that the prescribed ideal of *Vanaprasthashrama*—that is, retirement to the forest for contemplation after acquiring education and living a full life—was in operation in India more than two thousand years before Thoreau conceived of his withdrawal to Walden Pond. Thoreau probably did not receive proper instruction in this ideal, because he actually went and did it—that too, without having first lived through the preceding phase of a householder's life. And what a let-down for Indian ideals that Thoreau should have returned from the forest! Similarly, neither his frugality nor his passionate appeal to "simplify" could be expected to raise a flutter in a country where for so long a large proportion of its inhabitants has been living at the barest level of existence.

But "Civil Disobedience" is another matter, full of the promise

---

17. Cited by Walter Harding, *A Thoreau Handbook* (New York, 1961), p. 200; also in his notes on Gandhi and Thoreau in *Thoreau Society Bulletin*, XXIII (April 1948).

of righteous heroism and virtuous reward, and modern Indian history overflows with variations upon this theme. As instances of large-scale disobedience, neither passive nor civil, multiply on the streets of contemporary India, we are forced to do some serious rethinking on the problem of how common practice has perverted principles which had once seemed glorious.

Meanwhile, now that Thoreau's debt to India has been placed beyond speculation[18] and Gandhi's debt to Thoreau has been extensively studied,[19] the proper reading of Thoreau by Indians may begin, perhaps, in Indian universities where American studies are in the process of being established as a distinct discipline. One hopes that academic study of Thoreau will not be led into the narrow paths that Whitman has lately been led into by our more determined scholars.[20] We shall have to read Thoreau not merely because he imbibed Indian influences but also because he is a significant author in his own right even apart from his affinity to India.

18. The Variorum *Walden* identifies over thirty references to India and things Indian. *A Week* possibly contains just as many.
19. For example: George Hendrick, "Thoreau and Gandhi: A Study of 'Civil Disobedience' and Satyagraha" (Ph.D. thesis, University of Texas, 1954).
20. For example: V. K. Chari, *Whitman in the Light of Vedantic Mysticism* (University of Nebraska Press, 1964); M. N. Wankhade, "Whitman and Tantrism: A Comparative Study" (Ph.D. thesis, University of Florida, 1965); O. K. Nambiar, *Walt Whitman and Yoga* (Bangalore, 1966).

Thoreau in Japan

Katsuhiko Takeda

KATSUHIKO TAKEDA is an Associate Professor at Waseda University in Tokyo. He has written books on recent American literature, J. D. Salinger, Japanese literature, the Nobel Prize winner, Kawabata, and even on Japanese advertising. His interest in American writers is evidenced by his translations of Salinger, Cheever, and Updike and by his numerous articles on a wide range of subjects, including many on American literature and others on Japanese-American literary relationships.

THOREAU IN JAPAN

To understand the position of Western literature in Japan, we must approach the matter first of all from an historical standpoint. This means starting back as far as the beginning of the Edo period. When Ieyasu finally established his Shogunate in Edo, he governed a relatively unified country. The arrival of Western influences had caused the Tokugawa administration to close the country, and since 1640, after the virtual exclusion of Europeans, only a few Dutch traders remained on a tiny island in Nagasaki harbor. In Edo, the Tokugawa shoguns set up a regime with some of the attributes of a modern dictatorship. There were controls on traveling, the military barons were required to maintain houses in Edo where their families became hostages, and the lower classes were organized into small groups which were held responsible in total for the misbehavior of their members. Even religion was put to the service of the government.

Commodore Perry, charged with making arrangements for the trade with Japan that would ultimately force her to open her doors to the West, arrived in Edo Bay with four ships in 1853, the year before Thoreau published his *Walden*. Perry came upon a nation that was ready for change. Insularity was, by the end of the eighteenth century, beginning to give Japanese culture a stale, warmed-over look. Art and literature were for the most part repeating old themes. And the Tokugawa shoguns had indoctrinated the nation with a code of ethics that seemed unchangeable.

The trade treaty with Perry set off a train of circumstances beyond the shogunate's control. In 1867 and 1868 the last of the shoguns resigned, his followers were subdued, and the victorious young Emperor Meiji moved from Kyoto to Tokyo. Edo thus gave way to Tokyo and the Meiji Restoration was accomplished.

The reign of Meiji, from 1868 to 1912, was predominantly a

time of opportunity for Japan, a time when the disciplines instilled under the shoguns could be put to use in furthering the modernization of Japan. Under the new emperor, Japan began to adopt reforms from the West. Protestant Christianity was introduced, and missionaries were permitted to reside in Japan and build churches. The first Protestant missionaries who had entered Japan at Nagasaki in 1859 had been kept under strict police surveillance and were forbidden to preach to the people. But propagandizing nevertheless took place, and as a result the first native Protestant convert was baptized in 1864. The first Protestant church was established in Yokohama in 1872, and in the following year the government lifted its edict proscribing Christianity.

Anti-Christian sentiment was not substantially abated, however, until the 1880's, when Japan realized that she lagged behind the West in her isolation and would have to import Western civilization wholesale if she were to catch up with the rest of the world. At a time when all things Western were being eagerly welcomed by the Japanese, Christianity was naturally carried in on the tide of popularity, and missionaries were increasingly welcome as representatives of the new civilization.

Under these circumstances, the introduction of Western literature and art was accelerated during the period. But because American literature was in its formative years, the Japanese were more interested in English, French, German, and Russian literature. Even so, a few works by American authors found their way into the country. The first was a translation of Longfellow's "Psalm of Life," done by Hohchi.[1] One year later, Franklin was introduced.[2] This was followed in 1887 by one of Bret Harte's works, and in the same year Poe's "Black Cat" was offered to the Japanese public, in translation

---

1. Senkenkoji (Tetsujiro Inoue), "Tamano O no Uta," ("Psalm of Life"), *The Hohchi*, (24 April 1882).
2. Kunihiko Yamada, *Kingengyokoroku* (*Autobiography of Franklin*).

of course by the Yomiuri.[3] Thoreau, it will be noted, was not included in this group.

From 1864 to 1912

It is still unknown when, where, and by whom Thoreau was introduced to Japan. It can, however, be supposed that by the 1880's Japanese students of English came to know his name at Kaisei School, later the University of Tokyo. In the list of textbooks at Kaisei School there was Francis H. Underwood's *A Handbook of English Literature* (1883), which was divided into "British Authors" and "American Authors." The latter included selections from *Walden*. This book was also used as a textbook in the Doshisha Girls' High School in Kyoto during the 1880's.

Underwood's anthology contained three passages from *Walden*, together with a brief biography of Thoreau. The three selections were "The Bean Field," "Berries," and "The Pond." The first appealed to the Japanese love of agriculture, the second to their love for solitude, nature, and the fruits thereof, and the third to their deep response to the changing of seasons in nature. All three passages were evidently chosen for their potential appeal to Japanese readers.

But we must remember at this point that literature itself was not yet a popular subject during the 1860's, the 1870's, or even the 1880's. During those decades the leaders of Japan had their hands full, just catching up with other more advanced nations in politics, economics, and military affairs, and there was little time left for literature and the arts. This does not mean, of course, that all Japanese were indifferent to literature. Political writings were, for instance,

3. Kôson Aeba, *Miyamagi* (*M'liss: an Idyll of Red Mountain*), *The Yomiuri* (31 August–16 September 1887), and Kôson Aeba, "Kuro Neko," ("Black Cat"), *The Yomiuri* (3 November–9 November 1887).

quite popular, and if "Civil Disobedience" or "A Plea for Captain John Brown" or "The Last Days of John Brown" or "The Death of John Brown" had been introduced, things might have been quite different. But Underwood's anthology took a different approach, and the press of the time paid no attention at all to Thoreau.

It was through an edition of Emerson, already known in Japan from a biography by Tōkoku Kitamura published in 1894, that the scholarly press came to recognize Thoreau. The book, a translation of Emerson's letters, was by Sohō Tokutomi. He was a student of Jō Niijima (1843–1890), the founder of Dōshisha University, a pioneer in Christian evangelical work, and a former student at Amherst. Under his influence, Tokutomi read Emerson—especially "The Poet"—in *Essays, Second Series*, and was evidently much impressed. Later he became a journalist of importance, establishing the Minyūsha Publishing Company. His translation of Emerson's letters came out in 1901 as *Emerson no Shokan*. In it there was a letter dated 3 October 1839 from Emerson to Carlyle, in which Thoreau's "Sympathy" was first introduced to Japan. Tokutomi wrote a note on Thoreau and his art of poetry. Though very brief, Tokutomi's mention of Thoreau was of importance in advertising him to the Japanese, because at that time Tokutomi and his group were the leading journalist-scholars in Japan. Immediately Thoreau's name became known to those Japanese who were anxious to acquaint themselves with Western literature, and five years later, in 1906, Masanobu Ohtani published *Representative Works* by Emerson (*Emerson Kessaku Shū*), which carried the address given by Emerson at Thoreau's funeral. This introduced Japanese readers to the idea that Thoreau was sincerity itself and that the example of his life might fortify conviction in ethical law. Thoreau's virtues were coming to be closely associated with those which the Japanese esteemed and sought to attain.

Tokyo Senmon School (founded in 1882), later Waseda University, played a greater role in modern Japanese literature than did any other university, and it was through its influence that the next step was taken in presenting Thoreau to Japan. In 1891 it had begun to publish a magazine, *Waseda Literature* (*Waseda Bungaku*), which nourished many young writers and critics. Takitarō (*Hōgetsu*) Shimamura, who was one of the editors of this magazine, became the editor of the *Encyclopedia of Literature* (*Bungaku Hyakka Zensho* [1909]). Shimamura had a profound knowledge of English, but evidently not of American literature, so he picked two young scholars for the part on American literature. They were Masao Kusuyama and Empa Okeya. Kusuyama wrote the part up to the Civil War, while Okeya wrote about the period which followed. In this encyclopedia there appeared one item titled "Emerson and His Followers" ("Emerson to sono gaku ha"), which dealt with Emerson and Thoreau. Okeya also wrote a brief outline of Thoreau's life. He regarded Thoreau as a hermit—a Japanese hermit such as Kamo no Chōmei (1153–1216), who wrote *Hōjoki* (translated as *An Account of My Ten-foot Square Hut*). In Chōmei's case, however, there was a strong element of pessimism since he had abandoned the world because of the stress of the civil war between the Minamoto and Taira clans. A passage from his writing, however, shows that he was not altogether unlike Thoreau: "The flow of the river is ceaseless and its water is never the same. The bubbles that float in the pools, now vanishing, now forming, are not of long duration: so in the world are men and their dwellings." Perhaps the differences, however, are more important than the similarities. It is true that Thoreau retired to a hut built by himself near Walden Pond but, unlike Chōmei, he did not intend to retire from the world; rather, he sought a way to live in the real world. Evidently it was difficult for the Japanese of fifty years ago to come to an accurate understanding of Thoreau's philosophy, even though he was known to students of the English language and literature. According to the book list at the main library at Waseda University, *Walden, Excursions in the Field and Forest*, and *A Week on the Concord and Merrimack Rivers*—all introduced by Okeya—were bought in 1908. So Thoreau was first looked upon—and imperfectly understood—as a poetic thinker; since "Civil Disobedience" and "A Plea for Captain John Brown" were unknown to the Japanese at that time, he was not recognized as the practical citizen.

An annotated translation of *Walden* appeared in 1911. This was published by Koichiro Mizushima as *Shinrinseikatsu*. It became a best seller. The first printing was on 12 July. Two weeks later a second printing became necessary, and in three weeks a third followed. The book was not without its eccentricities—the Japanese could not pronounce English names correctly and Mizushima even wrote "Toroh" by mistake—but it was important because of its popularity and because of its preface. The preface was by the famous English scholar, Isoo Yamagata, and his observations are still of interest. In essence he noted that in the Meiji period the Japanese were apt to believe that the Americans put high value on material things and disregarded the inner life. This was not so. Had it not been for their high esteem for the spiritual life, the Americans could not have achieved so great a success in their civilization. So Yamagata asserted that the greatness of America depended upon such thinkers as Thoreau. Since Yamagata's time, the myth of American materialism has not altogether disappeared, not even after World War II. Some of the intellectuals who studied in Europe insist upon the superiority of European culture over American. Their grounds are poor: they merely repeat the old argument that America is new but Europe is old. This tendency was most common during the rise of nationalism after the Sino–Japanese War of 1894–95 and the Russo–Japanese War of 1904–05. Despite such prejudice, more in vogue during his time than in our own, Yamagata never failed to state the truth as he saw it.

In 1912 *A Chronicle of Thoreau's Words and Activities* (*Thoreau Genkō Roku*) was published by Kojiro Nishimura. This book resembled *The Thoreau Calendar* edited by E. M. Evors. According to Nishimura, Thoreau was the founder of the cult of the simple life rather than merely the poetic hermit as he had been characterized earlier. This same view was perpetuated in one of the articles of a contemporary journal written in English. The author, Shioya, was most interested in Thoreau's life of seclusion; also, he was apparently seeking oriental influences in American literature. Of *Walden* he said, "Walden is the crystalization of his personal experiences. The minutest observation of nature and the penetrating impression of it expressed in the beautiful descriptions are comparable to the beauty of Lowell's poems." The magazine, after the publication of a series of Shioya's papers, also published "The Site of Thoreau's Life in the Woods," an article which made use, for its cover, of a picture post card which had been brought back by a Japanese who had visited Walden. Thoreau, introduced as a poetic hermit, was coming to be known as a great thinker who espoused the simple life.

Between Two World Wars

World War I afforded Japan a chance to increase her position as a world power. In the international world she welcomed membership in the League of Nations. But economically Japan was becoming weaker and weaker. Militarists, taking advantage of the crisis, made their power strong enough to govern the country. From nationalistic motives, they rather unwisely rejected foreign influences. Just before World War II the people at large were deprived of freedom of speech as well as of publication. During the war everything was governed by militarists who ignored Western cultures. So studies of Thoreau came to a standstill. But it was evident that some sincere students continued secretly to conduct research in American literature.

In 1917 and 1919 the English magazine, *The Rising Generation* (called *Eigo Seinen* and which still exists), inserted an article on Thoreau with some pictures. The title was "Life in the Woods" ("Rinkan Seikatsu," XXXVII, Nos. 4–12 and XXXVIII, Nos. 1–2) and the author was Sakae Shiotani. In 1917 there appeared two essays on Thoreau—"On the Occasion of the Centennial Observation of Thoreau" ("Thoreau no Hyakunen Sai ni Saishite") in

Gokyō for 20 July (a publication of a Buddhistic group), and "Notes on Thoreau" ("Thoreau no Kotodomo") in *Bunmei Hyoron* for September. The first paper was written by Yu Funabashi. One of the earliest Americanists and a specialist in Whitman, Funabashi had graduated from the Aoyama Gakuin University and subsequently studied at Albion, Syracuse, and Boston. In his paper for the Buddhist society, he described Thoreau as a philosopher and religionist, but he did not regard him as a great writer. The other essay bears the name of Kokkeishi, but no one knows now who he was. The contents are a fragmentary description of the life of Thoreau, and they point mainly to the fact that the existence in America of a man like Thoreau tends to discredit the prevailing belief in American materialism.

Izumi Yanagida translated *Walden* in 1920 under the title of *Shizen Jin no Meisō*, which means "The Contemplation of a Man of Nature." This book was part of the fourteen-volume Tolstoy Memorial Library series, edited by Takeo Arishima and Roan Uchida. Mizushima's translation of 1911 had not been complete, so Japanese readers could now read the whole of *Walden* through Yanagida's edition. Judging from the introductory note to this book, we find that Yanagida regarded Thoreau as a philosopher rather than a writer. The word "Shizen Jin," a man of nature, suggested to the Japanese that Thoreau had in common with Japanese writers at least one of the traits or characteristics with which they were usually associated. Since they were apt to turn their backs on the world and live a quiet life contemplating nature, Japanese readers presumably found it easy to transfer their understanding of their own writers to Thoreau.

In 1921 *Walden* was translated by Kazuo Iwai and published by the Shinchō-sha publishing company, one of the biggest in Tokyo. The publisher gave the book such publicity that it ran into several impressions in a short period. Around this time young people began to take up camping, and a number of camping grounds were opened up in various districts in Japan. *Walden* became the Bible for this group and young campers read it avidly. Although this phenomenon seems to have been somewhat apart from a true appreciation of the literature itself, Thoreau's fame spread throughout the country.

Kinsaku Shinoda, professor of Tokyo University's College of Education, edited an excellent textbook version of *Walden* in 1922. This was one of the books in the *Kenkyūsha English Classics* series which every university, every college, and every library acquired. The books in the series were often used as textbooks. Shinoda wrote a detailed introduction and added appropriate notes so that the students could read and appreciate *Walden* in the original.

Shinoda, through his notes and comments, made two contributions to the understanding of Thoreau in Japan. First of all he pointed out parallels that led later scholars, like Hiromich Yahagi of Taisho University, to take up studies of the relationships between oriental writings and Thoreau's. He brought in comparison, for example, between Thoreau's thoughts and their oriental sources when he showed that the following passage came from *such and such* in Mencius: "You govern public affairs; what need have you to employ punishments? Love virtue, and the people will be virtuous. The virtues of a superior man are like the wind; the virtues of a common man are like the grass; the grass, when the wind passes over it, bends" (page 419). Secondly, Professor Shinoda acknowledged Thoreau's sincerely democratic attitude, especially as it was expressed in antipathy towards slavery. He praised Thoreau for living up to his principles, he dealt with the John Brown episode in detail, and by doing this he introduced one important but previously overlooked aspect of Thoreau to the Japanese.

In 1926 the young emperor Hirohito succeeded to the throne, taking as his title Shōwa. Soon after his coronation a great economic depression occurred. Widespread distress and unemployment led the Japanese intellectuals to reconsider national progress since the Meiji Restoration. They realized that though their predecessors had made efforts to transplant western culture into Japan, they had succeeded only in imitating it. Imitation in itself may not be wrong as a means of introducing a foreign culture, but if the imitators have no real understanding of what it is they imitate, the success of the process is bound to be limited. So during the early Shōwa period (1926–1939), Japanese intellectuals, although under the control of the militarists, really sought to understand the essence of American culture. This movement induced Yoshirō Kawazu to read Thoreau carefully. In 1928 *English and English Literature* (*Eigo to Eibungaku*), a monthly magazine edited by Kawazu, made its first appearance. His interest in Thoreau is shown by the fact that between July 1928 and August 1929 he contributed eleven essays on Thoreau to the journal. The emphasis was upon Thoreau's simplification of life, art of living, philosophy, love of freedom and nature, and artistry—altogether a rather extensive and sympathetic portrayal.

Whenever Emerson was introduced, Thoreau was sure to be mentioned as his follower. Tanosuke Hattori wrote a book in 1929, *Sacred Philosopher, Emerson* (*Seitetsu Emerson*), one chapter of which was allotted to Emerson and Thoreau. He praised both of them for their high principles of independence and veracity, pointed out elements of Indian philosophy predominant in the thoughts of both, and, influenced no doubt by Western literary scholarship, pointed out that both of them had used the works of Novalis, Marcus Aurelius, Spinoza, Descartes, Pascal, Schelling, Goethe, Montaigne, Saccas, Porphyry, Swedenburg, Duns Scotus, Thomas Aquinas, St. Augustine, Wordsworth, Browning, Shakespeare, Whitman, T. Parker, and others. Hattori's work no doubt strengthened the tendencies of the Japanese to regard Thoreau as a philosopher.

The first biography of Thoreau to be written in Japan appeared in 1934. It was based on the several earlier works by Emerson, Channing, Page, Sanborn, Salt, Allen, and E. W. Emerson. The author was Akira Tomita. In Part I, "The Days of Thoreau and Transcendentalism," he explained the background—romantic revolution—in which Thoreau was brought up and which influenced his lonely life. In asserting that Thoreau's denunciation of slavery was the result of his New England heritage, Tomita may have been guilty of historical determinism, but he did, nevertheless, help young students to locate Thoreau in relation to American literature and culture.

The most interesting section of the biography itself, Part II of the book, is that in which it is explained how and why Thoreau gave up composing poems and devoted himself instead to prose. Tomita translated Mrs. Lucy Brown's letter of 8 September 1841 to Thoreau, and he mentioned Emerson's advice that Thoreau turn to prose. This was, incidentally, one of the many places in the book in which Thoreau's debt to Emerson was discussed.

In "Thoreau as a Literary Man," Part III, Thoreau's style and sources were examined in detail. This study helped to stimulate Japanese readers to study American authors and it also introduced them to the comparative approach. The principal criticism which Tomita ventured was that Thoreau was defective in musical expression, this in spite of Thoreau's many references to music in *A Week* and elsewhere. It is curious, also, to find that Tomita suggested that Thoreau lacked concentration on his art. About Thoreau scholarship of the time there was still an air of naïveté.

Walden, translated by Seitarō Furudate, was published in 1933 as one part of a complete series of world philosophers. The series had a large market in Japan and ran through edition after edition, so Thoreau, in association with it, came to be more widely known as a philosopher. This tendency was extended in 1935 when in a biographical work, *Thoreau, the Man of Nature* (*Yajin, Thoreau*), Ryoho Horii treated his subject as a philosopher rather than as a writer.

The study of American literature apart from English literature began in Japan in the latter half of the 1920's. Several books on the history of American literature were published for the first time then, and Thoreau came to be evaluated and understood more in reference to American literature. The earliest of such books, *The History of American Literature* by Matsuo Takagaki (1927), devotes five pages to Thoreau, defending him from the allegation that he was anti-social, and explaining why it was that he was not understood and appreciated by his own contemporaries in New England.

In the 1930's there were two more histories of American literature which dealt with Thoreau. The first, published in 1932 and entitled *America Bungaku Gairon*, was by Tadaichi Hidaka, a professor at Waseda University. He simply identified Thoreau as a lover of nature whose romanticism was derived from transcendentalism. The second work, published in 1935 as *America Bungaku Taikan (Biographical Studies in American Literature)* was written by Kazuo Seki, also stressed the connection between Thoreau and nature. Further, it viewed his attitudes on society uncritically, and it even sought to disassociate Thoreau and Emerson. In its introduction, J. V. Nelson of Kansas University wrote that "Thoreau was looked down upon by some as an imitator of Emerson. This was reasonable for Emerson's philosophy greatly influenced Thoreau's thinking. But Thoreau's individual personality, his careful descriptions of the natural world, and his colorful humor far excelled Emerson in those aspects" (p. 80).

Academic studies on Thoreau started with Michio Tachikawa's "Thoreau and Walden Life," in *Aoyama Studies in English Literature*, a publication of the English department of Aoyama Gakuin University. The year was 1934. Two years later one of the most eminent scholars of American literature, Gen Sakuma, a professor at Waseda University, wrote "Notes on Thoreau" ("Thoreau ni tsuite no oboegaki") for the December number of the journal *Tankō*. This did much to clarify Thoreau's position in nineteenth century American literature. Between the world wars we find only two other academic studies. One was "An Introduction to Thoreau" in *The Rising Generation* (No. 6, 1939), written by Henry S. Canby, and the other was "Thoreau at Concord" ("Concord no Thoreau") in *Albion* (Nos. 4–5, 1940–41), written by Yoshitake Tsuruna. Since the Japanese military rulers suppressed studies of literature in America and England during these years, these two brilliant papers were read and appreciated by only a small number of Japanese. Although the academic studies of this period were superior to studies of any sort which had come out during the Meiji period, Thoreau's social documents had still not come into their own. In Japan, the people at large were not allowed to criticize the government and "That government is best which governs least" or "That government is best which governs not at all" were strictly forbidden statements. So in spite of the people's interest in these ideas, it was not until the end of the second World War that they came to be permitted and understood in Japan.

Thoreau Revival After the Second World War

Since the end of the second World War, American literature has been popular in Japan, both with specialists and the public at large. Although contemporary writers were most eagerly read, those of earlier periods were also studied since they provided the background to the moderns. As might be expected, Thoreau made a new appearance, and he was read along with Hawthorne, Emerson, Whitman, Steinbeck, Hemingway, Faulkner, Salinger, and others. The interest in products of the West was like that of the Meiji era except that during that period literature had been introduced to further Christianity while during the period following the war, literature was introduced to expose the Japanese to democracy. Also, the paperbacks which the American soldiers brought in had a great influence on the Japanese. American popular writings, good as well as trashy, were introduced uncritically and indiscriminately. Although Japanese society was somewhat restored by 1947, there was still a severe depression and the publishing business was in serious straits. Only 4,659 new books were published in 1946, and 5,484 in 1947. The figure increased to 26,063 in 1948. Every publication was under the strict control of G.H.Q., and in addition there was a severe shortage of paper and a serious lack of equipment.

Under these circumstances, *Thoreau no Kotoba* (*Thoreau's Words*) by Masaru Shiga came out in October of 1947. Shiga had a profound knowledge of American literature and made excellent choices from Thoreau's writings. For the first time in Japan, passages from "A Plea for Captain John Brown" and "The Death of

John Brown" were translated into Japanese. Thoreau was presented by Shiga as a writer rather than a hermit. To extend this image, he even included translations of some of Thoreau's poems.

In 1949 Akira Tomita, the author of the first biography of Thoreau published in Japan, translated "Civil Disobedience" into Japanese. It was published as a part of the famous Iwanami Library. In the introduction, Tomita praised Thoreau as a democrat and liberalist who had never submitted to authority. Japanese under democratization measures read this in the effort to better understand democracy. In effect, Thoreau had finally been brought outside of literary circles and introduced to ordinary citizens.

Much has been done on Thoreau since the second World War—up to 1962 there were eighteen translations, fifty-four scholarly papers, and twelve textbooks—so it is not possible to discuss everything. The two best works, however, are Rikutaro Fukuda's "On Thoreau" in his book, *The Portrait of American Literature (America Bungaku no Shōzo)*, and Masayoshi Higashiyama's *Studies on Thoreau*. Fukuda's original criticism focused upon Thoreau's literary style, a style, according to Fukuda, which Thoreau had learned from the Greeks. He stated that Thoreau far excelled Emerson as a stylist, although his prose, at its best in his paragraphs, did not grow beyond them. His style was simple and modest, yet abundantly suggestive. If at its worst it was sometimes monotonous, at its best it was pure, clear, free of excesses, and exemplary. In these respects, claimed Fukuda, there was no writer in American literature comparable to Thoreau. Stylistic criticisms of this sort and source studies of the kind done earlier by Hiromichi Yahagi have done much to advance knowledge of Thoreau in Japan.

Masayoshi Higashiyama, a student of American literature, devoted half of his life to the study of Thoreau. Presently the president of the Japanese Thoreau Society, he has recently published *Studies on Thoreau*. The most interesting of his studies is "Thoreau: A Japanese View," published at Kwansei Gakuin University in *Journal of the Society of English and American Literature* (No. 13). He says, "For anyone whose eyes can see what is going on in this evil world and whose brain can understand what his eyes have seen during the two wars, it would be difficult to accept Thoreau's opinion that 'That government is best which governs least' or 'That government is best which governs not at all.' Since the age of Franklin Delano Roosevelt, the role of government has become much more important and significant in our lives than it had been before. It has become our belief that unless social and international security are established, the freedom of individual beings is always in crisis, and that unless force backs us up, we cannot maintain a world of justice."

In conclusion it must be said that the study of Thoreau has been far behind that of Emerson or Whitman. One of the possible reasons is that early scholars considered Thoreau a philosopher and hermit rather than a creative writer; in addition, he was neglected by the popular press and consequently was not known to general readers. But as the war came to an end and the Japanese sought to understand American politics and culture, he came to the fore. Now that American literature is no longer regarded as an adjunct to English literature, the proper climate finally exists and much can be expected. The Japanese Thoreau Society, founded in 1965 through the efforts of Masayoshi Higashiyama and George Saito, will doubtless be responsible for much that is done in the future.

Thoreau in Australia

Joseph Jones

JOSEPH JONES, a native of Nebraska, has been a member of the English staff of the University of Texas, Austin, since 1935. He is a graduate of the University of Nebraska and holds the Ph.D. from Stanford. After a Fulbright assignment to New Zealand in 1953 (and other overseas teaching in South Africa, 1960, and Hong Kong, 1965), he became progressively concerned with "World-English" literature and has worked principally in that field both as scholar and teacher over the past ten years or more. His books include *The Cradle of Erewhon: Samuel Butler in New Zealand* (1959), *American Literary Manuscripts* (1960), *Terranglia: the Case for English as World Literature* (1965), *Handful of Hong Kong: a Visitor's Verses* (1966), and with Mrs. Jones as collaborator a forthcoming series under the general rubric "People and Places in World-English Literature" (single volumes on Canada, the West Indies, Africa, Asia, Australia, New Zealand). He is also editor for the World-English section of Twayne's World Authors Series and retiring editor of *WLWE Newsletter* for Group 12 of the Modern Language Association. Believing with Thoreau that "steady labor with the hands, which engrosses the attention also, is unquestionably the best method of removing palaver and sentimentality out of one's style," he spends as much time as he can in his woodworking shop.

THOREAU IN AUSTRALIA

When one enquires what Thoreau had learned about Australia, travelling much in Concord by means of books, the answer must be "Not very much." There is the occasional reference such as one to "the outlandish Australians" in the concluding chapter of *Walden*, where ridicule is poured liberally upon various exploring ventures including "that South-Sea Exploring Expedition, with all its parade and expense"—i.e., the Wilkes expedition of 1838–42. And in "Life Without Principle" there are several no less sarcastic paragraphs on the gold-diggings at Ballarat and Bendigo (in addition to those of California), with which Thoreau was made acquainted by William Howitt's *Land, Labour and Gold; or Two Years in Victoria*, more than likely through the Boston (Ticknor & Fields) edition of 1855. About New Zealand he must have been somewhat better informed by reason of his friendship with Thomas Cholmondeley, who visited Concord in 1854 and 1858 and whose *Ultima Thule* was published in 1854, the same year as *Walden*. Closer acquaintance in all probability would not have served to modify the unfavorable impression gained from Howitt. Socially and economically, Australia was not Thoreau's kind of a country—but neither was the one he lived in, for was not California (and Australia, equally guilty by gold-grubbing association) "the child of New England, bred at her own school and church"?

At the same time, Australia and New Zealand alike have furnished examples of naturalist-philosophers who fit after one fashion or another the Thoreauvian mold—omitting however the first European naturalist to see and describe either region, as one who would hardly qualify. This was Sir Joseph Banks, who accompanied Captain James Cook on the memorable first voyage to the South Seas, with some "parade and expense," in the late 1760's. Sir Joseph, long president of the Royal Society and the great scientific panjandrum of his day, was never the solitary type. It was he, nevertheless, whose observations and enthusiasm drew continuing attention to the unique natural history of the South Pacific and for whom the shrub *Banksia* and the Banks Peninsula of South Island, New Zealand, were named, not to overlook also Botany Bay. Through Banks, and others like him onward into the earlier nineteenth century, including Charles Darwin, the botany and zoology of the region received a reputation which had much to do with attracting later observers.

Thus we find, for instance, in the Hawke's Bay district of North Island, New Zealand, a farmer-naturalist named Herbert Guthrie-Smith whose attitudes towards the land, its products, and its inhabitants both human and animal, as expressed in his book *Tutira* (1921 and subsequent eds.), are distinctly in Thoreau's vein. Similarly, a South Islander of more recent days, Oliver Duff (*A Shepherd's Calendar*, 1962), might be mentioned. But it is an Anglo-Australian, born shortly before the publication of *Walden*, whose career offers the most striking parallel. Edmund James Banfield, "The Beachcomber" of Dunk Island, lived out a Walden experiment for twenty-five years and lies buried under an inscription from Thoreau.

I

Banfield was born in England in 1852, just at the beginning of an age of expansion for Australia through extensive gold discoveries that sent him there with his parents at an early age. He entered journalism and at length made his way up into Queensland where he worked fifteen years for the *Townsville Daily Bulletin*. During this period he made a return trip to England, where at Liverpool he met his future wife (They were married in Australia in 1886). After overwork leading to a breakdown in 1897, Banfield and his wife together with an Irish servantwoman took up residence on Dunk Island, two and a half miles off the Queensland coast about sixty miles south of Cairns—an irregularly-shaped island with an area between three and four square miles and somewhat over ten miles of coastline, rising in places to just under a thousand feet. Here they lived until "The Beachcomber's" death in 1923. He was "perhaps, a combination of Gilbert White and Thoreau," observed his friend A. H. Chisholm in 1925. (Mr. Chisholm, now a patriarch among Australian historians, recently reported in a private letter: "Incidentally, I was flown up to Dunk last month [April 1967]—my first visit since B's death—to unveil a memorial portrait, which is to be a central exhibit in a museum of Banfieldiana, and of course I saw the quotation from T. on the cairn above the grave.") Banfield continued to contribute to the *Townsville Daily Bulletin*, and after ten years' residence was persuaded by a visitor to Dunk Island, Sir Walter Strickland, to undertake a book: *Confessions of a Beachcomber* (1908). This was followed by *My Tropic Isle* (1911), *Tropic Days* (1918), and the posthumous collection *Last Leaves from Dunk Island* (1925).

Apart from his books, the most tangible memorial of Banfield's association with Thoreau adorns his island grave (which also contains the ashes of his wife, who died on the "mainland" in 1933). Mr. Chisholm writes:

> A cairn has been raised above the grave, and on it are words of Thoreau, words which the Beachcomber both loved and lived: "If a man does not keep pace with his companions, perhaps it is because he hears a different drummer. Let him step to the music which he hears" (*Last Leaves*, Introduction, xxvi. Photographs of the cairn appear opposite pp. 212 and 220).

This quotation had appeared on the original title-page of *Confessions of a Beachcomber*, together with another from Longfellow—"Trust in yourself and what the world calls your illusions"—which might just as well have been from Thoreau, or Emerson. The *Confessions* concludes, also, with a quotation from *Walden* ("Higher Laws"): "If the day and night are such that you greet them with joy, and life emits a fragrance like flowers and sweet-scented herbs, is more elastic, more starry, more immortal—that is your success." This climaxes a section headed "And This Our Life" (pp. 334-36) which would serve as a summary of Banfield's position. All four books abundantly reinforce such associations, both through direct reference and through the blending of acute nature-observation with introspection, social comment, and above all, humor. Re-cast from selected contributions to the Townsville paper, they are isotopes of a single substance: Dunk Island in all of its aspects which one observer was capable of recording.

In writing of *My Tropic Isle* Banfield distributes his emphasis pretty evenly among all three words of the title. He is proud of its insularity, its isolation; he praises it for the convenience its tropical location offers; he glories, somewhat tongue-in-cheek, in posing as its benevolent despot and preserver. Dunk Island affords him not only a profuse tropical vegetation, together with bird and animal life to observe, but in addition a great wealth of sea-life: sharks, rays, "curious bivalves," corals, crabs, sea-cucumbers, fishes of every description, and all the incredible marine phenomena of the Great Barrier Reef. He observes animal play and combat, reporting at length (Chap. IX) a fight between a lizard and a death-adder. Not wishing to neglect the human element, he interests himself in the personalities and activities of the aborigines much in the same way as Thoreau did in "Winter Visitors and Former Inhabitants," except that winter never came to Dunk Island (though hurricanes occasionally did) and the native inhabitants remained, much to the "Beachcomber's" satisfaction and amusement.

Banfield was "spiced and quickened by the sun of the tropics," says Chisholm, "so that he wrote engagingly of the wonder and beauty of his demesne—with an occasional excursion (as in *Tropic Days*) into the realm of Imagination—and accumulated a mass of valuable observations, including several discoveries new to science." Continuing, Chisholm measures him briefly against Thoreau:

> In sooth, Banfield worked at agriculture and domestic and semi-public duties as diligently as did Thoreau—was he not his own magistrate, postman, architect, carpenter, painter, boat-builder, goatherd, and the rest?—and yet contrived to improve upon the American recluse by being frankly human, and by keeping more or less directly in touch with the fretful world.

> He had his books, one or two newspapers (which Thoreau despised) and his English and Australian periodicals. For a *quid pro quo*, he wrote continually and amiably for all the world to read. Much of this work was in the form of fugitive articles, and, not being adaptable to book-form, will not be reprinted. On the whole, though, the quality was commensurate with the quantity; and the quantity was considerable (*Ibid.*, p. xxiii).

Some forty years later the Australian literary historian H. M. Green offered a more extended comparison. While somewhat reluctant to undertake "comparisons between Australian and world figures [which] usually mean little," Green concedes that "with Banfield, as the first and practically the only Australian example of a school, the comparison seems in place," even though it may prove "superficial and far too flattering from a literary though not from a human point of view." He continues by observing that there was "nothing of the hermit" about Banfield:

> It seems to have been love of fresh air and freedom and tranquility and dislike of the hurry and complications and trivialities of the modern world, together with the fascinations of this particular island, that caused him to live the life he did. He was neither eccentric nor self-centered but a balanced and normal person, with a strong sense of humour; he was also brisk and energetic, always busy at one thing or another: he did not, like Thoreau, sometimes, sit in his "sunny doorway from sunrise till noon, rapt in a reverie," though he could loiter when the mood took him; on the other hand he was not a thinker as Thoreau was, and he was by no means a master of style. (*History of Australian Literature*, p. 790).

This estimate is more just than not, but it could be argued that Banfield actually does approach Thoreau when we set him against the less polemic and philosophic, more relaxed and casual parts of *Walden* or *A Week*. In both Green and Chisholm we encounter the not-uncommon view of Thoreau as recluse and quasi-misanthrope, based upon selective reading of *Walden* and perhaps not much else.

Banfield himself makes such a selective use of Thoreau to reinforce some of his own beliefs. Writing in *Last Leaves* of a "homely garden" built near the beach where "taking a hint from Nature . . . water and sandy humus, enriched by the deposition of the refuse of ages, were available," he expatiates upon the virtues of natural soil, then offers a quotation together with his own parallel views:

> "Alas for human culture!" exclaims Thoreau. "Little is to be expected of a nation when the vegetable mould is exhausted and it is compelled to make manure of the bones of its fathers." Was this thought in the minds of the authorities when the regulations against the careless use of fire were issued subsequent to the cyclone? Was it recognized that in the jungle country fire would destroy not so much fallen timber as the very life of the soil, the result of ages of vegetable decay? Here in the North lies the biggest deposit of "last year's nuts." No other area within our borders possesses such an accumulation of the spoils of the past; and it is the duty of the individual, if not of the State, to safeguard the elements of the soil which are liable to destruction by fire (*Last Leaves*, pp. 50–51).

Other quotations from Thoreau include epigraphs to chapters four and five of *My Tropic Isle*, though it should be noted that such epigraphs include also a preponderance of English writers (Shakespeare, Byron, and Milton with two each, along with two quotations from Milton on the fly-leaf, and singles from Addison, Spenser, Thomson, Pope, Tennyson, Coleridge, and others). Thoreau is the only American author so honored, and there is very little reference to other Americans within the text of the several books.

More to the point, perhaps, are such passages as do not quote directly but rather show themselves as having absorbed and transmitted (and transmuted) Thoreau's ideas along with some of his tone. Here is an example from Chapter II ("A Plain Man's Philosophy") of *My Tropic Isle*:

> In such a scene would it not have been wicked to have delivered ourselves over to any cranky, miserly economy or to any distortion of affectation of thrift? Had fortune smiled, her gifts would have been sanely appreciated, for our ideas of comfort and the niceties of life are not cramped, neither are they

to be gauged by the narrow gape of our purse. Our castles are built in the air, not because earth has no fit place for their foundations, but for the sufficient reason that the wherewithal for the foundation was lacking. When a sufficiency of the world's goods has been obtained to satisfy animal wants for food and clothing and shelter, happiness depends, not upon the pleasures but the pleasantness of life; not upon the possession of a house full of superfluities but in the attainment of restraining grace.

It might be possible for us to live for the present in just a shade "better style" than we do; but we have mean ambitions in other directions than style. Style is not for those who are placidly indifferent to display; and before whom on a comely, scornful Isle shall we strut and parade? "You and I cannot be confined with the weak list of a country's fashions," for do we not proclaim and justify our own? Are we not leaders who have no subservient, no flattering imitators, no sycophantic copyists? The etiquette of our Court finds easy expression, and we smile decorously on the infringements of casual comers (pp. 31–32).

Echoes of *Walden* abound in this passage. Chapter IV on "Silences" and Chapter VIII on "Reading to Music" (bird music) might be similarly cited, as also portions of Chapter VI, "His Majesty the Sun," dealing with clothing ("The Tyranny of Clothes" had already received attention in the *Confessions*, pp. 171–72). Finally, a brief passage from Chapter VII ("A Tropic Night"):

As I gaze into those serene and capricious spaces separating the friendly stars I am relieved of all consciousness of sense of duration. Time was not made for such ecstasies, which are of eternity. The warm sand nurses my body. My other self seeks consolation among the planets.

"This huge stage presenteth naught but show
Whereon the stars in secret influence comment."

A grey mist masks the winding of a mainland river. Isolated blotches indicate lonely lagoons and swamps where slim palms and lank tea-trees stand in crowded, whispering ranks knee-deep in dull brown water. The mist spreads. Black hilltops are as islands jutting out from a grey supermundane sea (pp. 83–4).

As for most readers, *Walden* was probably for Banfield the staple. There is an occasional suggestion of wider acquaintance, as for instance in *Tropic Days* the use of a phrase, "The Scene-Shifter," to head a section in Part I (pp. 51–54), recalling the latter part of "Sunday" in *A Week*: "The Scene-Shifter saw fit here to close the drama of this day," etc. Banfield's reluctance to "parody" Thoreau was set forth explicitly in *Confessions of a Beachcomber*—

> It may have been anticipated that I would, Thoreau-like, set down in details and in figures the exact character and cost of every designed alteration to this scheme; but the idea, as soon as it occurred, was sternly suppressed, for however cheerful a disciple I am of that philosopher, far be it from me to belittle him by parody (p. 44).

—and he did not indulge extensively in direct quotation, as if to imply, quite properly, that the parallel must speak for itself. It does so, with singular eloquence, and in a context singularly well suited to the extension of the *Walden* experiment to ten times the original two years and two months.

*

Of lesser stature than Banfield, but similar to him in many respects, was a friend and fellow-journalist from Victoria, Charles Leslie Barrett (1879–1959). Since Barrett was a peripatetic "hodman of science" as he called himself—a newspaper-naturalist writing for the Melbourne *Herald*—he figured at times as a bush-guide for visiting biologists and consistently as a general "walkabout" reporter of Australian wildlife. Mr. Ian F. McLaren (*Biblionews*, August 1960) states that the period between 1920 and 1950 "saw an outpouring by Barrett which is probably unique in Australian literary writings." This outpouring included a series of "Sun Nature Books," beginning in 1932, some of which sold over 100,000 copies. Barrett also wrote juvenile fiction and capitalized upon travel outside Australia (to Egypt and Palestine, for example, during World War I).

Barrett's associations with Banfield are set forth at length in *On the Wallaby* (i.e., "on the loose in the bush," with or without specific mission, or in search of casual work), published in 1942:

> I envied him his serene island life. He surveyed the outside world through loop-holes of retreat, without ever desiring to return to it except as a visitor. His books will keep his memory green. Nothing quite like *Confessions of a Beachcomber* and *My Tropic Isle* has been written by any other author, I would give a whole row of romantic South Sea island books for one as sincere, as modest, and as pleasant to read as the amateur Beachcomber's *Confessions* (p. 162).

His own credo appears at the end of the same work:

> If my life could be lived over, I would still go on the wallaby in quest of wild beauty, of birds, and orchids, and of "small deer"; would go among blackfellows and seek for relics of the lost tribes (pp. 202-3).

And his credentials as Thoreauvian drop naturally enough into an amusing report of an *ad hoc* lecture:

> It is pleasant to recall the dismay of a girls' school principal, who had invited me to address her pupils, when I arrived after a long walk through the bush. The good spinster had read, in the local paper, about a young naturalist from the South who was bird hunting around Walgundra [Queensland], and had written asking the editor to book him for a Nature study lecture. No fee, of course—but the honour! For fun, I accepted. The girls were delighted, for I faced them in bush garb: khaki shorts and jacket, open-necked blue shirt, and mud splashed boots. My hair was unkempt. In brief, I looked the vagabond from head to foot, while the school, to a girl, wore spotless sub-tropical evening dress. An ordeal for the principal lady; yet I must say that she *was* a lady, not showing for a moment her distress at having introduced a "sundowner" into the exclusive school. My talk went over pretty well; for at least I knew my "ekker" as a naturalist. Besides, I was cunning enough to quote Thoreau and reel off a stanza from Tennyson's *In Memoriam* (p. 19).

Early in this century Barrett, who had already become acquainted with Thoreau, joined with two young companions in leasing a bark hut near Olinda Creek, some thirty miles east of Melbourne in the Dandenong country. This they christened "Walden" (its erstwhile name had been "Modesty Cottage") and formed themselves into a club, the "Waldenites." Writing as "The Woodlanders" they contributed a series of articles during 1905–6 to a Melbourne monthly, *New Idea*, in which they described the pleasures of occupying "Walden" during weekends and vacations. Devoted chiefly to ornithology, the series is extensively illustrated with photographs of birds, nests, and eggs, but it does offer a good snapshot of the bark hut itself and several of one or another "Woodlander" shinning up a tree or crouching in a blind for close-ups of bird life. Barrett's reminiscent account in *Koonwarra: a Naturalist's Adventures in Australia* (1939) offers these particulars:

> Rent, provisions, and railway fares; plates for the camera, books, tobacco; and sundry odds and ends, cost us from £1 to 30s. weekly. We led the simple life at Walden Hut.
> Why was it done? The Doctor said: "We'll spend all our week-ends and holidays at Walden; ramble all over the place; watch birds, collect plants; and make notes on everything. Then we'll write articles for magazines. Make a pot of money. I tell you, fellows, it will be wonderful. There's a book in it, Chas."
> . . . Having our city jobs to hold down, neither the Artist nor the Scribe (my Walden title) could spend weeks at a time in the country. The Doctor enjoyed more leisure, but must keep his practice going. So we gave to the Hut and bush rambles only long week-ends, and the annual month's vacation. Unlike our Master, we paid taxes, having no Emerson to pay them for us; and also, we welcomed visitors, which Thoreau seldom did. Solitude makes no appeal to normal youth. . . . Among our visitors were distinguished naturalists from other countries; artists, writers, a poet or two, and occasionally an editor. You see, we did write for the magazines and newspapers; Walden Hut became known, if not famous, though all that we valued was published in natural history journals (pp. 33–35).

Seeking counsel from W. H. Hudson about the "book in it," the

Waldenites were told: "My only advice to you, and to any man, is that of Thoreau—'follow your own genius.' Go on finding or making opportunities as you seem to have been doing already, in having a 'Walden Hut,' and probably in other ways" (*Ibid.*, p. 34). "That letter," says Barrett, "encouraged us to continue our Simple Life experiment—on the instalment plan." And it might be added that the Simple Life on the instalment plan is not altogether foreign to the pattern of *Walden* itself: Thoreau, as well, had "several more lives to lead, and could not spare any more time for that one."

*

A third figure of this same general period was Jack McLaren (1887–   ), the eldest son of a Melbourne clergyman, who became a bush-wanderer as well as something of a trader-entrepreneur in New Guinea and other Pacific islands. In 1911 he began a residence of eight years among the aborigines of Cape York, North Queensland, after which he returned to Sydney and Melbourne and at length migrated to London to become a writer of adventure stories (*The Devil of the Depths, The Money Stones*, etc.). Three autobiographical works—*My Odyssey* (1923), *My Crowded Solitude* (1926), and *My Civilized Adventure* (1952)—were all published originally in London and, in part at least, written there. The second, *My Crowded Solitude,* related how after some searching around Cape York peninsula for a suitable hermitage and coconut plantation he settled at Simpson's Bay with his stores, tools, and personal gear. Having cleared a site he built a hut—watching the work of termites during lulls in his own labors—and began making friends with the natives, some of whom he induced (for pay) to help with coconut culture. He received various visitors (an ornithologist, a gold-prospector, and others) along with letters from many parts of the world seeking advice on how to go about establishing oneself in a tropical hideaway. McLaren describes himself as an avid reader (*My Odyssey,* Chap. V), but inasmuch as he virtually never mentions or quotes literary works it is not possible to enroll him along with Banfield and Barrett as a "dinkum" Thoreauvian, however much he may have fit the pattern at times. He does serve quite well, though, to amplify the picture of the tropical recluse already established in the wake of R. L. Stevenson's residence in Samoa and of accounts by still other Australians such as Louis Becke. Queensland and the Great Barrier Reef appear to have offered the best local opportunities to assay the lure of the tropics.

Students of the Australian ethos (broadly interpreted) might see, in the behavior of such figures as we have been describing, a manifestation derived from earlier social, or a-social, patterns: the swagman "on the wallaby," the fugitive convict, the bushranger, perhaps even the aboriginal compulsions to the solitary "walkabout." While this is not the place to speculate extensively in such directions, there is considerable evidence to suggest that the opportunities, at times indeed the inescapable necessities, of solitude were abundantly present in Australia. So were they, for all that, in Thoreau's America; and we know that there were other Waldens than his. We should probably insist that to match the archetype, all such ventures ought to have been voluntary ones, involving an inborn preference for simplicity and independence coupled with a bent towards nature-observation and reporting. The Australians we have met, thus far, are fairly good representatives of the type.

II

Banfield's and Barrett's was not quite the earliest attention to be given Thoreau by Australians, although it may well have been the earliest indication of a pervasive influence. In the 1880's and 90's, the more "radical" of mid-19th century American authors still held considerable appeal for Australian radicals of various persuasions, most particularly those campaigning for political independence. Whitman especially found favor; and it was Whitman who most attracted an Irish immigrant journalist named Thomas Bury ("Tom Touchstone" was the pseudonym under which Bury wrote weekly columns for the Ballarat *Courier*). In turn, Bury transmitted his enthusiasm to a young poet named Bernard O'Dowd, who for a time corresponded with old Walt in Camden and who wrote and spoke voluminously on his behalf. Bury was a vegetarian, and in his newspaper columns occasionally cited Thoreau together with numerous others as evidence for the virtues of a vegetarian diet. He speaks, for instance (*Courier*, Oct. 27, 1888), of the "wonderful and immortal book *Walden*." It was Whitman, however, who claimed his chief allegiance.

Also in Victoria, at Melbourne, there was a lively "freethinking" movement coupled with schisms in the churches. One such produced the "Australian Church" of the Rev. Charles Strong, a single but rather large and vocal Melbourne congregation which was founded in 1886 after Strong had broken with the Presbytery following some nine years of progressively stormy service in the Scots Church. The *Australian Herald*, as the organ of this sect (if one congregation can be so designated), printed frequent articles on socialism and social reform, carrying also literary notices and biographies. Among American authors mentioned and quoted with some frequency by this periodical were Emerson, Lowell, Whitman (the subject of a series by the *Herald's* chief poet, William Gay), Holmes and Whittier. The issue for December, 1891, carries a two-page sketch signed "J. M." entitled "Henry David Thoreau, the Concord Hermit. 1817–1862, Aged 45."

The purpose of "J. M.'s" short essay, apparently, was to offer Thoreau as still another example of the independent personality willing to think for himself, and to praise him as a "master phrasemaker, [who] wrote purest English." It begins by observing that "Individuality was strongly marked in Henry D. Thoreau; he was a *character*, resisting to the full that tendency of society which reduces all to a flat surface." Thoreau is called the "Yankee Diogenes," "western Socrates," and "our present day St. Francis," with Emerson's funeral tribute quoted as reinforcement. The Walden experiment, with related short excerpts from *Walden*, forms the core of what is said, but the reader is reminded that "the two years' life of Thoreau at Walden has been exaggerated; it was merely an incident, a curious and interesting one, in his life and a very natural outcome of his thoughts and habit." (At one place, nevertheless, it is stated that "Thoreau was a *hermit* of the woods," as the title of the article implies.) Similarly in the apologetic vein is a statement that Thoreau was "a poet, whose lyric gift was not great, but still a poet," and another:

> That he was a crank some may hold; if so, he was of the kind described by O. W. Holmes—one who made the wheels of the world *go round.* Who would not be such a crank? It may be said if the world were peopled with Thoreaus it would be a strange world. True; but the strangeness would soon disappear, for he was a bachelor. But who will name the one man to be accepted as the type of all, who should fill the world, so that it should not be a strange world? Surely that's an impossible task.

Brief reference is made to Thoreau's interest in the "Bibles of Oriental nations, and Plato's works"—not likely to be stolen from his cabin, so "what need to lock a house whose treasures were [these]?" The concluding paragraph reads:

> In an age when men are being levelled down to a common type, we should be thankful for the originality, the *inner* resources, the simplicity, the crystal purity of life and thought of Thoreau. If we hesitate about the first part of Browning's prayer, "make no more giants, God," we say a fervent amen to the second petition, "*Elevate* the race, at once." Thoreau is not a giant; but he has power in him to elevate.

*

It seems evident, then, that such attention as Thoreau received in Australia during the latter 19th and earlier 20th centuries was sporadic but occasionally quite intense, as with Banfield. He was known, along with his American contemporaries, as the "right" kind of an author for a young, ambitious people. Although active Australian nationalists turned more naturally to those with a political outlook of cleaner cut, Thoreau's idealism still carried weight. Some were content to take him in his capacity as naturalist-philosopher; others, following at a distance the lead of British reformer-socialists (who were prominent in what might be termed a kind of Thoreau revival at the end of the century, and whose republication of "Civil Disobedience" reached Gandhi in South Africa), found what they needed in his social polemics.

III

We come now to *Bellbird Eleven: Life in the Woods*, by Derek Robert, published in London in 1965. The author is a professional sailor, whose previous books—*Look at Me Now* (1963) and *That's the Life for Me* (1964) describe adventures around Australia and in other parts of the Pacific. In one sense, then, Robert may be taken to be (in American terms) a kind of hybrid between Melville and Thoreau, or (in British terms) an offshoot of Conrad with something of the philosophic "Marlow" in his outlook. *Walden* infuses his third book so extensively, however, that it no doubt must be regarded as one of the most resolute of all attempts—from Australia or elsewhere—to "parody" Thoreau, recalling Banfield's disclaimer. Its chapter-heads as well as its subtitle make clear this intention at a glance.

No small part of the charm of *Bellbird Eleven* lies in its Thoreauvian mixture of earnest with irony (the latter element implied in the very title itself, which was the author's telephone number "in the woods"). We are offered a semi-dramatic personal narrative in which the author, tired of the sea, comes ashore. After finding no sympathetic haven in an Australian city, he purchases a small tract of land (fifteen acres) with a barely habitable small house on it in a rural backwater below Geelong, sixty miles southwest of Melbourne and not far from the Southern Ocean. Here he relaxes for some months, acquainting himself with his neighbors (including brute neighbors—possums, termites, stray sheep, crows, magpies, a few derelict chickens, and a stray cat), reconstructing and furnishing his house, and commencing to discover and relish various sights and sounds. Chapters entitled "Where I Lived," "Neighbours," "Laws," "Solitude," and "What I Lived For," belonging to this period of novitiate, already are patterned *à la Walden* (the author's phrase, used later). We are assured, however, that Robert had never read Thoreau before he took another summer hitch at sea in order to acquire more needed capital for his Bellbird venture.

Halfway through the book, then Thoreau steps personally onto the stage. Aboard the *Donnybrook* of the Southern Hemisphere Steamship Company, a passenger cruise-ship, Robert by a happy chance finds *Walden* in the ship's library. "By the time the ship reached its paying-off port I was as familiar with *Walden* and Henry David Thoreau as it is ever possible to be with a person who has been a century in the grave" (pp. 88–89). From this point onward —through "Economy," "Labour and Leisure," "Visitors," and "Housewarming" to at last "The Break-up"—the parallels become deliberately conscious, quotation abounds, and there is a running debate, not so much over the merits of the *Walden* way of life (which is taken to be all but axiomatic) as over its serious feasibility in our day, even at Bellbird.

Robert admires Thoreau at least as much as did "J. M." or "The Beachcomber" before him, calling him "old master" and loosely imitating his tone and style. *Walden* becomes the Bellbird Bible ("In the evenings I would sit by the bougainvillea in the cool air and read *Walden*," p. 111); and other works by and about Thoreau find their way to his small book-collection. The contrasts between Concord township and Bellbirdshire (as still, for all its seclusion, vulnerable to modernity—and so was Walden in the 1840's) are many, and astutely rendered.

Robert writes with a lively sense of metaphor and successfully avoids the pitfalls of pedantry as well as of self-gratulation. He also has a novelist's eye and ear for the revealing episode and for dialogue. In a week-long conversation with a visitor identified as Jean-Jacques (an Anglo-French cousin, resident in Australia as one of the engineers on the great Snowy Mountains power and irrigation scheme), the issues of society vs. solitude are hammered out. It is tempting to offer protracted quotation from this, and from numerous other sections of *Bellbird Eleven*, but I will not risk dulling the pleasure that many Thoreauvians will undoubtedly come to take in this most pleasurable book. Nor will I detail the bacchanalian events of the "housewarming" (which some critics might label "typically Australian") leading shortly to "The Break-up." The reader should hear, however, the two final paragraphs:

> I doubt that Thoreau is dead at all. Hardly a week goes by that I do not come across his name in a paper or a magazine or a book which I open. It was as if his remark had come true: "What you seek in vain for, half your life, one day you come full upon all the family at dinner. You seek it like a dream, and as soon as you find it you become its prey."
> And so I become a prey to Thoreau's concept of life. It lies in wait for me when I make these hitherto unexpected rendezvous in the printed word; they remind me of my rights and duties—and how much I am failing in them—all the time; they have renewed my hope. Adieu, Bellbird! I now return to the great workhouse of the world (p. 182).

*

To have fossicked out these "parallels," "influences," and such, is mildly interesting as part of the scholarly game we play; but I know that what remains so largely unsaid is the most important of all—and not for Australia alone but for all the sporadic "documentary" reticulations of Thoreau's influence and image that a book designed like this one is able to touch upon. It would take many pages—another *Walden* or more, in itself—to explore expressions of the Australian mind in an attempt to discover how *Walden* still echoes without tangible reference to itself; without having even consciously touched this writer or that one, so far as we can tell. Its issues touch us all, at one place or another, so that when an Australian poet like Robert D. FitzGerald declares

> . . . I count this gift
> priceless: that I have been
> never so far adrift
> from cliff, creek, ravine

>   and red gravel of the ridge
>   that from my youth on
>   I could not find some ledge
>   neighbourly to the sun. . . .
>   ("Strata")

we murmur "Thoreau" to ourselves without knowing or necessarily caring overmuch about direct associations. The same would hold true for such a book as Douglas Stewart's *The Birdsville Track*, or the poetry of Shaw Neilson, or Randolph Stow's *To the Islands*— or for much that we find in Judith Wright, Herbert Guthrie-Smith (across the Tasman), or Bernard O'Dowd. Still, we can take rude bearings from *My Tropic Isle* or *Bellbird Eleven*—benchmarks a generation and more apart—into the larger territory where the particular dissolves into the general, and the special concerns of literary history merge with ever-continuing concerns for the condition of man. "That was a more pertinent question," says Thoreau (in "Life Without Principle"), "which I overheard one of my auditors put to another one—'What does he lecture for?' It made me quake in my shoes."

Principal Works Cited

Edmund James Banfield, *Confessions of a Beachcomber* (London, 1908). The title-pages to three editions of *Confessions* . . . available in the Grattan Collection of South Pacificana at The University of Texas form an interesting contrast. The original, as mentioned, carries quotations from Thoreau and Longfellow; the Appleton edition ([New York, 1924] "Printed in Great Britain" and done apparently from the plates of the London original but omitting the greater part of the illustrations) carries neither; and an Australian edition ([Sydney: Angus & Robertson, 1933] somewhat abridged) retains, in italics, the "drummer" quotation from Thoreau but omits Longfellow. Mr. C. Hartley Grattan purchased his copy of the latter at Tully, North Queensland, just before embarking for a visit to Dunk Island.

Last Leaves from Dunk Island (Sydney, 1925).

My Tropic Isle (London, 1911).

Tropic Days (London, 1918).

Charles Leslie Barrett, *Koonwarra: A Naturalist's Adventures in Australia* (London, 1939).

On the Wallaby (Melbourne, 1942).

Robert D. FitzGerald, *Forty Years' Poems* (Sydney, 1965).

H. M. Green, *A History of Australian Literature* (Sydney, 1961).

William Howitt, *Land, Labour, and Gold; or, Two Years in Victoria*, 2 vols. (Boston, 1855). (First published in London. Howitt was the one source of Thoreau's information about Australia, as confirmed by John Aldrich Christie's *Thoreau as World Traveler* [New York, 1965], which offers no evidence of further reading.)

J. M., "Henry David Thoreau, the Concord Hermit. 1817–1862, Aged 45. *The Australian Herald* ([Melbourne], December 1891), pp. 86–87.

Derek Robert, *Bellbird Eleven* (London, 1965).

Henry David Thoreau, *Works*, ed. H. S. Canby (Boston, 1946).